Nothing is as precious or as fragile as m those memories detail a time no longer tied to the living or even to a physical setting. As Southerners, we still spend an inordinate amount of time telling the uninitiated about our home places, groping for words and examples which "tell the truth" to incredulous listeners. But how do we tell the truth with love and humor when we know the depths of despair behind the comic stories or eccentric characters? Jimmie Moomaw has told the whole story of her "Southern Fried" childhood in Brookhaven, Mississippi, and she does it with delicacy, hilarity, love, grief, and sharp insight. In a day when memoirs can be classified into one of two categories: dysfunctional childhoods or ancestor worship, Jimmie writes the whole story of loving parents whose little girl was the center of their emotional universe and of the alcoholism both wrestled with all of their lives. Flawed, but determined to give Jimmie her dreams, her parents are remarkably creative.

There are sharp and vivid vignettes of dozens of people who peopled Jimmie's childhood, some clearly eccentrics, like Lulu who has a son named Elvis Presley Junior Smith and who claims to be able to cast devils out of kittens, or Miss Dorothy the spectacularly toothy elocution teacher whose pupils gamely attempt to recite her favorite poetry with dramatic flair, but who only manage to be "what you'd get if you had a bunch of wind-up toys who could recite Byron, Shelley and Keats." There are the nuns--- Mother Superior Freida whose "*ethos* was awesome; fierce, pious, patient, unbending, innocent, yet omniscient." And young and pretty Sister Clare, the kindergarten/piano teacher "who was the only nun [Jimmie] ever saw lift up the skirts of her habit a little bit and skip like a child." There is Jimmie's Uncle Frank (married to Jimmie's mother's second cousin) who owns the local funeral parlor, the May sisters who beautify the women of Brookhaven (including regularly frying Jimmie's hair with a "hot perm") while wearing their own hair in bowl cut coifs, and a scrawny, choir robe clad thirteen year old who enjoys burning down churches and half of Brookhaven for weekend entertainment. There are many more.

Don't miss this vibrant, funny and poignant memoir of a Southern childhood. If you liked *Angela's Ashes* and *It's All Over But the Shouting*, you'll love *Southern Fried Child*.

Dr. Bridget Pieschel Smith, Director of Women's Research and Public Policy Institute at Mississippi University for Women; Formerly Director of Welty Writer's Symposium; author of *Loyal Daughters: One Hundred Years at Mississippi University for Women 1894-1984*.

Southern Fried Child
in Home Seeker's Paradise

JIMMIE MEESE MOOMAW

authorHOUSE®

AuthorHouse™
1663 Liberty Drive
Bloomington, IN 47403
www.authorhouse.com
Phone: 1-800-839-8640

First published by AuthorHouse 9/7/2010

ISBN: 978-1-4520-6406-2 (e)
ISBN: 978-1-4520-6404-8 (hc)
ISBN: 978-1-4520-6405-5 (sc)

Library of Congress Control Number: 2010912384

Printed in the United States of America

This book is printed on acid-free paper.

For My Daughters: Betsy and Amy

To help you know and understand and remember,
and because I so wish my Mama and Daddy
had written one of these for me.

Acknowledgements

It would never have occurred to me to write a journal that turned into a book about my southern fried childhood had I not been inspired by reading a journal my cousin, Hazel Martin Howell, made in a creativity class.

There would have been no reason for me to begin writing had I not wanted to leave a log of memories for my children, Amy Fleming Goodnight and Elizabeth Meese Peyton and my precious grandchildren Nellie, Crawford, Jamie, Wyatt and Emmaline.

By giving me their "quality time" before anyone had ever heard of such a thing, Mama and Daddy together helped me love to learn. Daddy taught me how not to stop at the easy quitting place. And Mama, the master "dream enabler" taught me to believe in myself. Even their flaws became my strengths and instilled in me the need to be fiercely independent.

After I finished the manuscript and needed tough, honest criticism, I turned to my friends, Dr. Virginia Kent Leslie, Dr. Nancy Forderhase, and Dr. Bridget Pieschel for help. Their comments and encouragement were invaluable. Special thanks to Michael Clements for design assistance with cover.

I am grateful to all the above for their role in bringing "Southern Fried Child" to fruition, but most of all I am indebted to the cast of characters who peopled my world growing up in "Home Seeker's Paradise" – Brookhaven, Mississippi – back in the 40s and 50s. Without the raw material of experiences I shared with them there would have been nothing to say.

June 11, 2010

Contents

Prologue

When my cousin Hazel Howell came to my daughter's wedding, she brought along a journal she'd made in a creativity class. When she read it to my children and grandchildren and me, I thought it was the most wonderful way to build a word bridge between generations and decided to make a journal of my own. I'd always felt that I could never really understand my own roots because neither of my parents were given to introspection and it would never have occurred to them to consciously and deliberately search their souls and share their insights with me. I, on the other hand, have always been a psyche-prober and wanted my children to know and understand and remember me.

That's how this book began. But it is not what it became. I'd always heard writers say that "something took over" when they started writing and they really didn't know where their pen would take them. That sounded like a lot of ouija board voodoo to me. I won't say I flat out didn't believe it, but I certainly didn't understand it. Until it happened to me.

I'd set out to write about Aunt Edna and wind up writing about Sister Clare and the nuns at St. Francis of Assisi. What began as a litany of the names of dead relatives, not unlike the pages of *begets* in the bible, evolved into a narrative account of things I did and people I knew as a child growing up in Home Seeker's Paradise (the marketing slogan for my hometown), Brookhaven, Mississippi. At some point, I *realized*, rather than *decided*, that the tone of the book had become markedly *southern fried* and that I was writing for general consumption rather than just for my progeny.

As I wrote, I discovered that memories are linked and chained. You capture one and pull on it and another one follows. Broad shapes take form and definition and details follow. Dreams are remembered along with deaths and pets and dangers and people and problems.

Sometimes I was fuzzy about exact dates – like *exactly* how old I was when a specific event occurred. Others I'm positive about. I have a receipt dated 1947 for $5.00 I paid on the watch I bought on credit for Mama for Christmas that year, which means I really was only ten years old when I worked as a cashier in Mr. Lankford's shoe repair shop.

As a Professor of Rhetoric and Communication, I always stressed the importance of organization and arrangement, but found that organizing the episodes of my life proved far more challenging than the classroom exercise. I just wrote an episode and then another and then another, and as I did, sets and subsets began to self-sort and cluster: dangerous things, first things, fears, friends, fish, family, pets – pain.

I must tell you too that I left out a lot. As an only child of alcoholic parents, I heard and saw much that was painful and ugly, much that I would rather not remember and cannot forget, but I chose not to dishonor the memory of my Mama and Daddy by going there, because there was also much that was good. Their love for me wasn't exactly unconditional (it was conditioned on my being a good and perfect child – or so I thought), but it was deep and undeniable.

I also found that some episodes played out over pages and

pages while others were just snippets, single events, little vignettes that couldn't be stretched into more than a few paragraphs.

All children should be given a camera as soon as they are old enough to use it and be taught to take a snapshot of everyone in their life that could be considered interesting, eccentric, unforgettable, fun or just plain crazy. I know I'd give anything now to have an album full of photos of the dozens of people in my hometown that made a cameo appearance in my southern fried childhood, though I have to admit that when I lived among them, they didn't seem so extraordinary. Only now in retrospect do I realize what a marvelously odd lot of people central casting put down in my home town in the 40s and 50s. Some, of course, like my parents and a few blood relatives played starring roles and were always near the center of my life, but there was also a remarkable parade of teachers, neighbors, friends, customers and assorted "town characters" who touched my life and left indelible marks. While the episodes presented here are recollections of experiences I actually had, I changed the names of several real people to avoid unnecessary disparagement, ridicule or embarrassment.

The toughest part of writing this was deciding on a name for the book itself. The episode titles came pretty easily. "Elvis Presley Junior Smith and Poot," for example, was really easy. A neighbor gave birth to an illegitimate son and called him Elvis Presley Junior at about the same time she bought a goat that she named "Poot" because he smelled so bad. Others like "How I Know For Sure Why I'm Afraid of Mice," "Dammit, Daddy, It Got Away," and "Shooting Stars and Sunset Carson" pretty much named themselves, but the big question remained. What should I call the book? I finally realized that when someone asked me what my book was about, I'd say "it's a book of "southern fried" episodic memories about my childhood." Thus, *Southern Fried Child*.

When applied to food, I guess *southern fried* literally refers to our tendency to roll chicken and pork chops and cube steaks and okra and green tomatoes in flour or cornmeal or some other kind of batter and fry the hell out of it in an inch or two of pure lard. More generally, it refers pretty much to any element of a diet that is associated with the South. Grits is the first thing that comes to mind. Along with boiled peanuts, fried catfish, and chitlings.

Connotatively, "southern fried" is an expression that refers to Southerness in a general and generic sense. If there is a uniquely Southern voice used to communicate about uniquely Southern experiences, and I certainly believe there is, then "southern fried" is my phrase for it.

Still, since I haven't lived in Mississippi since the early 60s, I was surprised when I realized that so much of what I wrote about was so "slap dab" Southern. That I wrote with a Southern drawl.

Almost every Mississippian I have ever known who "left home," and that includes not only those who left the state physically and literally, but also those who "stayed put" at home but left behind the mores and values of their fathers and mothers, has at some point become introspective and contemplative about his or her root experiences. So I guess it should have come as no surprise that I was no exception and that when I began to remember and write, I wrote not in the voice of the academic I grew up to be, but in the voice of the southern fried child I once was.

At first I tried hard to maintain a purely narrative/descriptive perspective, choosing to avoid the introspective, reflective posture typical of "enlightened" Mississippians – both those who return only in memory to their own southern fried childhood and those who come home only for the rituals – for funerals and weddings and to visit graveyards and the ever-thinning ranks of their childhood friends and distant relatives.

But maintaining a purely narrative perspective turned out to be very hard to do, and I didn't completely succeed. As I remembered, I became reflective in spite of myself. Finally I stopped fighting it and said to myself, "You're a girl, named Jimmie, the only child of alcoholic parents. You were born in the Deep South before *Brown vs. Board of Education*. If that isn't enough to make you reflective, then you have absolutely no capacity for introspection."

Let me tell you something else. You might be tempted to believe that the Gothic characters you see in the movies with the bad, bad southern accents are the products of the alcohol induced dementia of failed novelists turned B-movie screenwriters, but the South I grew up in *was* peopled with characters like Lola in "An Epitaph for Lola." They walked into and out of my Daddy's little country grocery store and service station every day of the week. People like them were the stuff of Truman and Tennessee and William and Willie and Eudora's fiction. They were the stuff of my every day life and reality.

I'll never know for sure who or what I might have been or would have been if I had been born in Connecticut or Detroit, but I am now sure that I am who I am in large measure because I was born in "Home Seeker's Paradise" and lived a southern fried childhood, complete with horses and healers and "heatherns" and whores and flawed parents who loved me both too much and not enough.

Etta Maye and Ella May

$\mathcal{T}$he two most significant women in my life from the day I was brought home from the hospital until the day I left home to go to college were Etta Maye Crawford Meese and Ella May Winston. They were both nearly six feet tall and big women – not fat – just big. Both had small bones with well turned ankles and small wrists, and each carried a barrel of weight on her torso. Both smiled a lot, laughed easily, were naturally nurturing and overtly affectionate and both called me *honey* or *darling* or *baby* until they died.

Etta Maye was my Mama. Ella May was always with us. She never married and never had any children of her own, and I still don't know what to call her. Our maid? Cook? Housekeeper? Babysitter? Nanny? Hardly. She was, in fact, all those things. She helped Mama around the house with everything from putting away the winter clothes to canning fig preserves and muscadine jelly. But she was so much more than that. She was my very best friend and I loved her with all my heart.

Mama was married for twelve years and had to have some kind of operation to help her get pregnant. She had a couple of miscarriages along the way before she was finally able to conceive and carry me to term. While Mama carried me in her womb for nine months, it was Ella May who met Mama and Daddy in the driveway when they brought me home from the hospital and carried me into the house and put me in my crib. Maye and May shared duties in raising me from that moment on.

Ella May didn't live with us. She lived in the "colored quarters" in a two-room unpainted shotgun shack next door to her Mama, Melissa. She had a great chinaberry tree and one red rose bush in her front yard, a rag tag vegetable garden between her house and Melissa's, and from time to time she shared her place with her long time boyfriend, Walter B.

She also partied and drank bootleg whiskey every weekend and Daddy had to go down and get her out of jail more than once. One time one of Walter B's other girlfriends cut her badly with a broken beer bottle, severing a tendon in her left bicep that left her with a floppy wrist over which she had little or no control.

Many times my Mama failed me. Disappointed me. Because of her drinking. Ella May never did. When Mama and Daddy left me at home to go out drinking, it was Ella May who stayed with me and played with me and prayed with me. She loved me and I loved her – as they would say now – unconditionally. She fed me, she played games with me, told me stories, took me for walks, and comforted me. She was the only other human on earth who really knew what it was like then in my house or how much it hurt my heart. And when I cried, she held me and hugged me and made me feel loved. Until after I went off to college, I didn't – or couldn't talk to anyone about my parents' problem. Not to anyone except Ella May.

She also taught me how to fight.

Those who know me as a contentious, stubborn, ornery, and sometimes combative adult may find it hard to believe, but there was a time in my earliest childhood when I was a timid little pacifist. In the very first house we lived in, we had a next door neighbor with a little girl only a bit older than I was. Her name was Nancy. Just to look at her you would think she was the best-behaved little goodie girl in town. She was actually a bully extraordinaire.

There was a wire fence between our backyards, and she tormented me through that fence every chance she got. I was too inexperienced at war games to realize if I stayed away from the fence, she couldn't get me, so I stupidly kept going back to the fence again and again, and every time I did that little "bad seed" attacked me again and again. Her three favorite types of violence were biting, pinching and spitting and she was skilled at all three, especially pinching, which she did so hard that her little fingernails broke the skin.

One day, after Nancy pinched me so hard she drew blood on my cheek, I ran crying to Ella May. She usually soothed and comforted me, but that day she had had it with Nancy. She picked me up, put me on her lap and explained war to me in very simple and direct terms.

"Baby," she said, "this here is lesson number one."

"In this world," she said, "you either hit or git hit. If you want to keep her from hurting you, you gotta hit her first. Next time she starts after you, don't run from her. Don't run to me. Just haul off and hit her."

Nancy and I both stayed away from the fence for a few days. Then one day she came over to my house ostensibly to play, but really so she could launch a more direct attack on me. We were on an enclosed back porch and there was a window between the porch and the back bedroom. Back then our windows didn't have automatic spring sashes and counterweights and the only way to keep them up once you opened them was to prop them up with a *window stick*.

Ella May gave us some colors and coloring books, told us to play "nice," winked at me and went back in the kitchen. Nancy smiled and nodded like the goodie girl she pretended to be when any adult was around.

Ella May was barely out of sight when Nancy grabbed for the color I had in my hand and at the same time tried to rip out the page I was coloring. I held on tightly to the prized red color, and expecting that a frontal assault was imminent, stood up and put it behind my back. Enraged by my unexpected resistance, Nancy was by this time hell bent, not just on taking my red color, but on inflicting some real misery on me. She scrunched up her face into a nasty little scowl, lowered her head and charged. This time, she wasn't aiming to pinch, bite or spit, she was going to head butt me – hard.

Suddenly, Ella May's words "hit or git hit" had real meaning. I decided she was absolutely right. I put the red color in my left hand and held it out in front of me to taunt her a little bit. With my right hand, I reached over and picked up the window-holding-up-stick and in one unbroken motion, raised it and lowered it, whacking the charging enemy right across the top of her head. I'm not sure whether I generated the force with my back swing, or whether her own forward motion carried her hard on the stick, but the meeting of stick and head produced a big "thwack" and a look of sheer astonishment from Nancy. She stopped, looked at me in total disbelief, sucked in all her breath, and held it until she was turning blue. Then she exhaled, started screaming and took off running.

I think she passed Ella May coming down the hall, but Ella May didn't stop to comfort her. She came straight out to me. She was smiling, and so was I. It was the first lesson, but far from the last lesson that Ella May Winston taught me.

Like Demosthenes Said. . .

*H*ave you ever noticed that grown-ups always ask kids the same three questions: "What's your name?" "How old are you?" and "Wha'cha wanna be when you grow up?"

From the time I got a blackboard and started playing school with Mama and Daddy until I got my first job filling in for a pregnant English teacher in West Memphis, Arkansas, I had the same answer to the third question.

"A teacher," I'd say, "I want to be a teacher."

Because Mama worked with Daddy at the service station he ran, Ella May kept on working for us, cleaning a little, cooking some, but mostly looking after me when I came home from school. She continued to be my best friend, my playmate, my surrogate Mama – and my first student.

At some point when I was in the third or fourth grade I began to notice that Ella May didn't speak as clearly and distinctly as I did. I'd read somewhere, probably in the "D" volume of my World Book Encyclopedia, that Demosthenes, an eloquent, famous, long dead orator had put pebbles in his mouth at the seashore and practiced speaking over the sound of the in-rushing waves to improve his diction. I decided that I could and should teach Ella May to do the same.

She seemed dubious about the process I described and about our prospects for success, but she agreed to do it, so we went out in the driveway and got a handful of gravel and brought it in and scrubbed it. Since we were a couple of hundred miles from the nearest beach, we turned on the radio to substitute for the sound of breaking waves.

I suspect that Demosthenes (if, in fact, any of the pebble story is true) just placed a couple of small smooth pebbles in his mouth. I insisted that Ella May put a handful of rocks in her mouth, and I turned the volume on the radio up high. In spite of her initial reservations, bless her heart, she gave it a really good try. While she sat there in front of the radio with her cheeks puffed out like a chipmunk looking serious and hopeful that in a couple of minutes she'd turn eloquent like Demosthenes, I realized I didn't know what to do next.

I told her to say something. That stumped her. She went blank and could think of absolutely nothing to say. Having her make up an original oration on the spot was clearly out of the question so I looked around and found an old copy of "Reader's Digest." I didn't think we should start with long words or foreign sounding words, so I read her a joke and told her to repeat each phrase after me. And she did, but, of course, with her mouth full of rocks, she had to try to keep her lips together to keep from swallowing them or spitting them out, so instead of increased clarity, she could barely mumble.

We both held it together pretty well until I got to the punch line. I don't remember what it was, but just say it was something like, "Whoa, goat, you gotta let the pig go first!" Then she said something like "Whuh doat, woo dotta det duh …," and we both lost it. I looked at Ella May and started laughing and then she looked at me and started laughing and when she did, she spewed gravel everywhere. I mean *everywhere* and that made us laugh even harder. When she got her breath and could talk again, we both swore that she sounded a lot better, but we never had another speech lesson and we didn't tell Mama what we'd done.

For days after that, Mama kept finding rocks in the strangest places and saying,

"Now, how on earth did that rock get under there?"

How My Daddy Really Said "I Love You"

When I was in the first grade, Sister Clare cast me as the head little angel in the Christmas pageant with lots and lots of lines to say. I think she did it because she thought I had the two talents requisite for a starring role in a St. Francis play – I talked loud and memorized fast.

Mama and Daddy were really proud that I was going to be an angel and say a lot of lines. Mama bought some white material that was soft and had a shiny thread running through it, making highlights sparkle under the spotlight. I also needed wings. St. Francis being a parochial school, every school play there had an angel and some kind of saints in it.

Most angel wings for costumes were just cut out of white poster board and tied on. Think about it. Keeping cardboard wings on a squirmy kid requires real engineering skill. Most angel wings were really flimsy, got bent or broken, and hung limply catawampus somewhere between the back of the neck and the butt. Greta Garbo would have been hard pressed to maintain her composure and portray an ethereal being with your average pair of homemade, grade school angel wings flopping around behind her.

From time to time, my Daddy did things so totally out of character that to this day I can't explain his aberrant behavior. His baseline behaviors were well established. Macho Meese man – tough. Son of Quaker Mama man – silent, stoic, emotionally repressed. Insecure man – heavy drinker.

I know that my Daddy loved me, probably more selflessly than Mama did, but he could not say the words – ever. Sometimes he'd look at me with so much love I thought he would "bust" wide open. He would look right at me with his ice blue eyes and an impish curl of a smile, and he'd wink at me and say, "I don't care nothing about you." Here inflection is everything. To a reader, the bare words on paper might seem harsh and cruel, but if you'd seen and heard *how* he said it, with that look and that smile, you'd know, as I knew then, those words meant the exact opposite. That was how my Daddy told me he loved me.

So when Daddy did something uncharacteristically unmanly, I was always surprised. Like sometimes, my Daddy, fighter of fires, greaser of trucks, re-capper of tires, would go into the kitchen, get out some pots and pans and *cook*. He had three specialties. When Mama and I went to church on Sunday morning, he'd cook lunch. Always the same thing – baked baby bream, little fish with lots of tiny bones that he covered with a wonderful sweet, hot, tomatoey sauce that I'll never forget and never be able to duplicate. Fried oysters. He and Mama loved them, and I loved the crunchy fried cracker crumb breading he rolled them in. And oddest of all to me was when Daddy made homemade pasta. He'd start from scratch, mixing eggs and salt and flour into a dough. Then he'd roll it out, cut it with a knife into long strings, put them on coat-hangers and hang them all over the kitchen to dry. I was positive that nobody else in Brookhaven had a Daddy who made homemade spaghetti. I never told anybody about him doing it though, because I wasn't sure whether I should be ashamed or proud that Daddy cooked. I suspected it had something to do with him being a Yankee.

Well, when I got cast as an angel, Daddy got aberrant again. About making my angel wings. The first thing he did was devise a wire hanger that Mama sewed into the back of the angel robe. Then he glued three or four pieces of poster board together to make them strong. He drew and re-drew a pattern for the wing shape until he had a pair of gracefully arching, perfectly symmetrical wings.

Any other parent would have stopped right there, but Daddy was going all out for realism. He bought a bunch of white crepe paper from Hoffman's Drug Store and started obsessively cutting out little individual feathers and putting them in an empty cigar box. When he finished cutting, he started pasting. One by one he glued down the base of those little crepe paper petal-shaped feathers so four-fifths of each one would stick up and flutter. He glued them down in over-lapping rows and tapered them from large to smaller as he moved from the base toward the tip. The whole contraption had some kind of wire attachment in the middle to stabilize it, so when he stuck it into the frame Mama had sewed into my robe it was kind of like plugging a light into a wall socket.

The finished product came about as close to real angel wings as a human man could make them. The Christmas pageant that year was one of the best St. Francis ever had. Everybody said so, and I remembered all my lines and said them loudly and with appropriate vocal emphasis, but what everybody complimented most were those angel wings Gordon Meese made for his daughter.

And that's how my Daddy really said, "I love you."

Half Yankee

*N*ot long after the Christmas pageant, Frankie Joe Loicano proclaimed his undying love for me. This presented a problem. Mama had always told me in that conspiratorial way mothers pull daughters aside and try to warn them about "boys" that I could tell her anything. Just come to her, she said, and I could tell her anything, and she wouldn't even be mad with me. No matter what it was. She always said it in a way that implied that I might as well tell her such things because somehow in secret ways known only to mothers of daughters she would know it any way. I was convinced that she could take one look at my face and know what I was thinking, and I'd already had the one and only spanking I had in my life for lying about cutting my leg with an egg beater.

Anyway, I guess Frankie Joe and I struck up some kind of schoolyard friendship. He was a new boy at school, and he was very cute. He had black hair and dark brown eyes and long curled-up eyelashes. He had a bunch of brown freckles smudged across his nose, and he smiled a lot. The details of how he came to proclaim his love for me have long been forgotten, but he did. He announced that I was his girlfriend.

As soon as he told me that, I was pretty sure that this was one of the "somethings" Mama was talking about when she said I could tell her anything. The other problem was that I had somehow learned that Frankie Joe's daddy was Italian, and I figured that might be the kind of thing that would make Mama and Daddy consider him unacceptable as a son-in-law. At that time, bigotry toward "foreigners" was deep seated and overt, less veiled than other prejudices that prevailed in the South.

When I got home that day and was alone with Mama, I told her I had something I needed to tell her. She knew from my tone that it was one of those serious things she'd instructed me to tell her about. She immediately stopped peeling potatoes, wiped her hands, sat down and looked at me, smiling a little apprehensively because she had no idea what I was going to say and could for a moment, I suspect, imagine all sorts of worst case scenarios.

I mustered up my courage and struggled to find the right way to tell her with just the right words and with just the right tone so she would understand that in spite of his *Italianess,* Frankie Joe was a really nice little boy and I liked him.

I'd always felt a little foreign myself since my daddy had been born in Danville, Illinois, and I was, therefore, technically half Yankee. I actually heard more openly derisive talk about Yankees in Brookhaven back then than about ethnic and religious minorities. Though Daddy drawled like everybody else so you couldn't tell he'd been born North of the Mason-Dixon line, I knew he was a Yankee and wasn't exactly sure where that put the Meeses in terms of social stratification, so what I said and said very quickly to Mama was, "Mama, I've got a boyfriend. His name is Frankie Joe Loicano, and he is half Italian and half white child, but he can't help it Mama – because, Mama, you know, I'm half white child and half Yankee."

As soon as I made my confession implying that Yankees weren't Caucasians, Mama couldn't keep her straight face any longer. She laughed and hugged me and laughed some more. I had no idea why she was so happy or what she found so funny about my reflection on my lineage, but it didn't matter. I loved to hear my mother laugh. She did it so well – and really so often.

I was just relieved. My burden had been lifted. Mother knew I had a half-Italian boyfriend, and she was happy. So I was happy. I was always happy when my Mama was happy. And always devastated when she wasn't. Unlike Daddy who lost his temper fast and got over it in minutes, Mama's bad moods lasted a long time and were manifest two ways. She had small lips anyway and when she was pouting she would pinch them together so tightly that she had almost no lips at all. Or she would look wounded and go off into another room and sorrowfully hum hymns. Not happy hymns or the ones they used in church to invite you to give your soul to Jesus, but the ones that were sung at funerals. The slow, mournful ones, like "The Old Rugged Cross" or "I Come to the Garden Alone." Mama knew I hated for her to pinch her lips and hum mournful hymns. She did it deliberately to torment me. To punish me. Really she did. If I did something to upset her, she went into her unhappy act because she knew I hated to see her pinch her lips. When I couldn't stand it any longer, I'd go up to her and say, "Please, Mama, please stop pinching your lips and humming."

I don't know why I bothered though, because it never worked. All it did was let her know she was really getting to me and that just made her keep on pinching and pouting and humming.

Crime and Punishment

The first "let's pretend" game I remember playing was "school." My Daddy, who dropped out in the 8th grade, and my Mama, who made it all the way through Martinsville High School before running off to marry Daddy, made learning fun by playing school with me every night after Daddy got home from the service station and ate supper.

For Christmas one year (1940 or '41), Santa Claus brought me a sandwich-board style blackboard and some chalk and we got serious about playing school. We assumed our roles with appropriate shifts in tone and demeanor, Mama and Daddy affecting childlike voices when they played students and I doing my best to lower my voice, wrinkle my brow and look appropriately grown up when I pretended to be the teacher. Mama would call out some numbers and Daddy and I would race to see who could add them fastest. Then the teacher would call out spelling words, and I'd break them into syllables and say them out loud and then spell them syllable by syllable.

"Teacher...tea-tcher. Tea...t-e-a. Tcher...c-h-e-r."

What we were playing was immaterial. What mattered was that Mama and Daddy *played* with me and made me feel loved and smart almost every night when they weren't drinking. I'm positive neither of them ever heard the phrase "quality time." I'm equally sure that playing school with my Mama and Daddy was the first link in the chain of probability that led to me becoming a teacher.

In spite of my play school accomplishments, when it came time to go to real school, according to Mississippi law, I wasn't ready because my birthday was on January 13, thirteen days after the cut off point for enrollment in a public school, so Mama and Daddy decided to send me to the Catholic school because they had the only kindergarten program in town.

Oddly enough, this led to my first experience with discrimination and bigotry. It was in my own family and had nothing to do with race. Aunt Edna, the Super Christian, attacked Mama's decision immediately and repeatedly.

"Maye, you're gonna be sorry. They're gonna turn that child into a CATHOLIC," she warned Mama with the tone of certitude that only the truly devout and self-righteous can assume. I knew when I heard her say it that she was predicting I'd be "turned into" something awful – something even worse than Lot's wife getting "turned into" a pillar of salt.

But I was proud of Mama. Aunt Edna was the big sister that she always looked up to and turned to for help and advice. They told each other everything, and in truth, Aunt Edna really was a model of tee-totaling rectitude. This time though, Mama didn't back down.

"No, they're not, Edna," she said, and held her ground.

And they really weren't. When the Catholic children had catechism for thirty minutes each morning, the nuns let me have free time to study, read, and do my homework. Aunt Edna's narrow-minded and dogma-driven attitude about Catholics just confused me. Since the teacher I simply worshipped and all my friends were Catholic and the smartest, sweetest, kindest, and most patient people I'd ever been around, I could not understand why Aunt Edna was mad at them, and I secretly thought that getting turned into one of them would be something to be proud of.

On Ash Wednesday when my Catholic friends got ashes rubbed on their foreheads, I told Sister Clare that I wanted some smut rubbed on me too and proudly went home to show my smudge to Mama. She didn't seem to mind at all. When I asked her if getting ashes on my head meant I had been turned into a Catholic, she just smiled and said, "No, you're still a Baptist," but I could tell she was glad that Aunt Edna didn't see my forehead that day because she'd have said, "I told you so, Maye. The next thing you know that child is gonna be praying to statues."

It was somewhat ironic that I became such a devout defender of my nun teachers, because before I started to school there I was scared to death by the very sight of nuns in their intimidating black and white habits. When Mama drove past the Catholic school and the nuns were outside, I'd lie down on the car seat and hide my eyes like I did when we drove across high bridges. I just wanted to make big bridges and penguin-people disappear.

In spite of my earlier fears, once Mama and Daddy enrolled me at St. Francis, I fell in love with all the nuns, especially Sister Clare. One day during the three months I was in the first grade, I got so carried away with love and admiration, I walked up to Sister Clare's desk, and before she could see it coming, reached up and kissed her on the cheek.

I'm telling you, you've never seen blushing until you've seen a virgin nun blush. Sister Clare turned crimson, almost a deep red purple, like a really ripe plum, but she kept on smiling and didn't scold me.

For the next two years, my life was inextricably interwoven with Sister Clare's. As my teacher, she weighed and measured me, evaluated my health, commented on my deportment, graded my ability to read, write, and do 'rithmetic, and recorded it all in her flawless handwriting on my report cards.

Because Mama still worked at the Pure Oil service station with Daddy, working the cash register and making charges in a little flip-page charge book, she was never home to fix dinner (the noon meal) and so they paid the nuns to let me, along with a couple dozen other kids, eat at the convent. We ate in a big sterile room around four or five big tables on floors covered with the kind of linoleum you'd expect nuns to choose. No one could have accused those nuns of worldliness or pride based on their choice of linoleum. If they could have, they would have covered the floor with linoleum that looked just like the floor it covered. Nothing decorative. Like everything else in the convent, the room where we ate was Spartan in concept and sparse in its execution. And really, really clean. But, somehow, when the room was filled with hungry Catholic children and a few little hungry Protestants, when the nuns quietly filled our plates with red beans and rice and white bread and butter, the whole place changed.

Disciplined and well-behaved children that we were, we didn't dare raise our voices. We did become quietly animated. In that room, beneath that cross with a suffering, sad Jesus hanging on the wall, we knew two things for sure – all the nuns loved us, and nobody could cook rice and red beans better than Sister Marie. They were so good that we didn't mind eating them almost every day, but did get excited when mashed potatoes replaced the rice and we had meat loaf. Of course, Friday was tuna fish and slaw day.

When we finished eating, we were allowed to go out and play for the rest of the noon hour. Trouble was, we didn't have much to play with. On the playground, there was a set of swings and monkey bars suspended from a really tall iron pole frame. The footing were supposed to be anchored in cement, but when I pumped hard and got those metal chains flying and pushed toward the sky with the soles of my feet, the frame of the swing set would pull up a little ways out of the ground making it feel like the whole thing was going to tip over. Rhythmically the pole, yielding to the momentum of my pumping, would rise like a serpent out of a hole in the ground, hesitate and fall back with a distinctive "thunking" sound. In this tug of war between physical forces, gravity always won and the swing set stayed standing until the old school was demolished and the playground modernized.

There was a flimsy sliding board by the side of the swing set and that was it. We had no other playground equipment. We did have an open area to play softball and a few medicine pins, I think they were called, though even then that seemed like a strange name for heavy wooden things that looked like old pins from a bowling alley – and a volley ball. The volleyball was the recreational toy of choice as it could be used not only to play volleyball, but also dodge ball, keep-away, and some truncated version of soccer. I'm pretty sure that no kid in Brookhaven had ever seen a real soccer ball or a soccer match, but it just seemed like a natural thing for kids to do. If you had a ball, you just wanted to kick it.

I got into big trouble because of that ball, or more precisely, because there was only *one* ball. For the whole school, K-7, we had one ball. Since the girls and boys didn't play ball together, Mother Superior ruled that boys and girls would take turns getting to play with the ball, and further that said ball would remain inside the school under lock and key until she came out and turned it over to the gender players of the day.

One day, when it was the boys turn and the ball was under lock and key but not heavily guarded as one might expect for such a valuable resource, I, for some still unfathomable reason, decided to disregard Mother Superior's ball rules and capture the ball for the girls. Some of my friends boosted me up so I could stand on the water fountain under the window of the classroom where the ball was kept. I stood on the fountain, pushed up the unlocked window and pulled myself through. Hardly a stealth operation, I freed the ball in broad daylight in front of virtually every girl at St. Francis of Assisi.

For one triumphant moment, I basked in the admiration of my co-conspirators who were either awed by my bravery or stunned by my stupidity. Then we literally took the ball and ran. Even the older boys were, I believe, surprised by my display of personal bravado. For some reason, they didn't try to use their superior numbers, size and force to retake the ball. I think they knew it would be more fun to watch us get caught than to take the ball back, so they were satisfied to taunt us with hoots and warnings.

"You're gonna be sorry! She's gonna get you!"

And sure enough, she did. Though I knew Baptists didn't have to go to confession every time we did something wrong, I decided that as a Baptist who had sinned in broad daylight in front of all the school-aged Catholic children in Brookhaven, I might as well confess. I was sure that even if I decided to stonewall it, a cover-up was impossible because at least one, and probably all the girls, would confess their complicity the first time they went to confession, and though I'd heard what you said in confession was confidential, I wasn't sure I believed it. I suspected that the first time the priest talked to Sister Freida he would tell her, "You know that ball heist last week – well, Ann Foggo told me Jimmie Meese did it."

All this having flashed through my mind after having captured the ball, but before Sister Freida discovered it, I decided to do the honorable and inevitable and confess. I really didn't have any choice. Even though in the eyes of the Lord and Sister Freida, I had *stolen* the ball, I knew I could never look sister in the eye and tell a lie.

You see, this was only a year or two after I had the one and only spanking I ever had in my life, and it was for lying. I found an old rusty razor blade and hid under the steps of the back porch and cut a long straight gash on my leg trying to shave my legs like

Mama did. I knew I wasn't supposed to play with a razor blade and when Mama asked me how it happened – I lied. But not at all cleverly or convincingly. I looked her in the eye and told her I cut it with the eggbeater, which I called a *zigzag*, so Mama took me in the bathroom and spanked me for lying. She spanked me until she was tired. Then Daddy took over. He gave up too, and Mama started over again before I confessed.

That first spanking experience was fresh in my memory, and the enormity of my sin was becoming clearer and clearer when Sister Freida opened the convent door, assumed her most imperial penguin pose, stepped off the porch and walked purposefully back to the school to get the ball for the boys.

Sister Freda always walked purposefully, her body language screaming, "You really don't want to mess with me!" That day I watched her closely and saw the exact moment she realized that the ball she was on her way to get out of the closet in her classroom for the boys was already on the playground, in the hands of the girls.

With her steel-trap mind, I knew that she knew. She knew that she hadn't gotten the ball. She knew it wasn't the girls' turn. And now, overwhelmed with a sense of sheer, raw guilt, I was sure she already knew that I did it. Co-conspirators began dropping like flies.

She stopped about thirty feet away from me and just stood there. She didn't move for what *seemed* like a good hour and a half. She didn't have to. She just looked at me, right in the eye. All my early fears of women in penguin costumes resurfaced. I can't even imagine anything more terrifying to a sinful child than being stared down by a pure and virtuous nun, whose very title, MOTHER SUPERIOR, marked her as the infallible ruler of the Catholic school children of Brookhaven's entire universe. She was the head penguin. She wasn't staring at Peggy Peavey, the oldest and biggest girl in school, or Bertha Lee Robin (who years later would become a nun herself) or Ellen Pond who was usually the first girl in school to get into trouble. Just me. She motioned for me to come. Subtly. Not with words, or even hand gestures, just with a slight, ever so slight, nod of her head.

I wanted to run to her, fall down at her feet and throw myself on her mercy and ask her forgiveness, God's forgiveness, Jesus' forgiveness, Mary's forgiveness, and the forgiveness of all applicable saints. I started walking toward her, wishing that I had listened to those morning catechism lessons that I was exempt from. I had no idea what the penance might be for grand volleyball theft. I didn't even own a rosary, but as I approached Sister Freida, I suspected that I had committed a sin so grievous that I might have to kneel down and pray to a statue. At that moment, if Sister had told me to, I would have, regardless of what Aunt Edna might have to say.

If you ordered a Mother Superior out of a Sears-Roebuck catalog, you'd get a Sister Freida. Tall, thin, straight as an ironing board, nun-scrubbed face with clear open pores you see only on faces never touched by Maybelline (or even a puff dusting of Coty's face powder), round un-rimmed owl-eye shaped glasses, eyes of an indeterminate color. Eyes that could talk.

I don't know what's happening in our genetic codes, but it seems to me a new breed of human children has evolved in the last sixty years. The children I see now running un-tethered and screeching like crows through public places can't be controlled by parents who try to compensate with double decibel volume for their lack of vocal authority.

Back then, Mama and Daddy and the nuns; in fact, any person tall enough to pass for an adult could control me with just a look. A piercing look, a slightly raised eyebrow, or in my mother's case, tightly pinched lips were commands. They all meant the same thing, either "be quiet" or "stop what you're doing – now." All the kids I knew were disciplined the same way.

Without saying a word, Sister Freida's *ethos* was awesome. Fierce, pious, patient, unbending, innocent, yet omniscient. And so stiff and starched and clean. Sister Freida would no more have thought of raising her voice to me than she would have watched "The Flying Nun" on TV, had there been TV in Brookhaven then.

She held my fate in her hands. I really believe that as she looked down at me and paused, that for a flicker of a second, just the slightest possible hint of a teeny, tiny smile slipped across her upper lip. I knew then that I would be okay. Behind that stern nun mask, I saw that Sister Freida was at least a little bit amused, that she still loved me, and on some sisterhood level that pre-dated the feminist movement by decades, she was proud that the girls got the ball, and in her pre-nun days she'd probably sinned like me.

She kept me after school for a week. But it wasn't a bad punishment. I got to spend more time with the nuns and see what they did when all of the students went home. I was surprised that they talked to each other like Mama and her friends when they played canasta (though certainly not about the same things) and that they laughed a lot. Out loud.

The Nun's Story

S ister Clare was the nun with the biggest smile. She was young and radiant. Her face always glowed like she had just finished scrubbing it. She laughed out loud a lot, and I adored her. While the nuns wore no distinctive ornamentation of any kind to express their individuality or call attention to themselves, Sister Clare stood out as a one-of-a-kind nun. Not only was she the youngest, prettiest, happiest, and sweetest nun I knew, she was the only nun I ever saw lift up the skirts of her habit a little bit and skip like a child. She was my kindergarten teacher, my combined first and second grade teacher, she directed the first plays I was in, she helped serve the lunches I ate at the convent, she was my piano teacher, and because we couldn't possibly get a piano up the stairs into our little one bedroom apartment, she was there to let me in and supervise when I went to practice on the piano at the convent.

It's ironic that I wound up taking piano from Sister Clare instead of speech lessons from "Miss Dorothy," Brookhaven's resident classical elocutionist, since I was awful at playing the piano and wound up earning a living talking and teaching talking.

One day Mama was sitting around with her friends, Cat and Irma, smoking cigarettes and drinking coffee in the "gossip box" at the back of Irma's little dress shop when Cat and Irma started talking about Miz So-and-So's daughter Sue Ann or Lou Ann or something. Cat Jackson, who had no children and Irma Foster, who had two sons but no daughters, were apparently quite impressed that Sue Ann or Lou Ann or something could play the piano, sing and tap dance like Shirley Temple and recite poetry and dramatic literature so well that Miss Dorothy said she was good enough to be a Broadway star. She was, they agreed, *"a very accomplished young lady."*

It was pretty clear that most of the families that lived on the two oldest tree lined streets in town – the ones where all the big old white antebellum houses rose out of patches of red and white and pink azaleas – had two goals for their children: to raise their daughters to be *accomplished young ladies* and get them married *before* they got pregnant, and to raise sons with a enough sense not to get caught in some *unaccomplished young tramp's* daddy trap.

Before that conversation, Mama had never thought about "turning me into" a *very accomplished young anything in particular,* probably because she knew that I was a poor prospect for accomplished young lady training, but she came home telling Daddy that I needed to learn to play the piano and tap dance and say poems out loud. Daddy was as surprised as I was about this turn of events. If he was trying to turn me into anything, it was into a very accomplished young fisher-child. They talked about it a little while (as long as Daddy talked about anything) and decided that they couldn't afford the cost of turning me into a full-blown accomplished young lady, so they'd shoot for turning me into a *semi* or *sort of* accomplished young lady. They gave me a choice – I could take piano from Sister Clare or elocution from Miss Dorothy.

Miss Dorothy was one of Brookhaven's legion of old maids.

Certainly the most flamboyant one. She had red hair so bright that it all but glowed in the dark and a whole lot more teeth in her mouth than her big lips could cover. She spoke with the dramatic intensity and affectation of a Broadway diva that marked her forever as a small town "wannabe" actress – who not only couldn't make it in New York – but couldn't make it anywhere else either.

Everybody in Brookhaven knew who Miss Dorothy was. I'd never met her, but I'd seen her around town a time or two. I couldn't believe that homely as she was, she walked down the street like she thought she was real pretty. And I'd never heard anybody that talked the way she did. Everybody – and I mean everybody else in town – drawled their words in varying rates of slow. Everybody prolonged their internal vowel sounds and didn't move their lips much at all. Everybody but Miss Dorothy and Miss Theresa Abshagen, the legendary senior English teacher at Brookhaven High School.

Miss Dorothy spoke every sound in every syllable of every word so distinctly that it was as if her words were nails and she was trying to bite the tips off of them. I was sure it was hard to talk like that with all those teeth and you did need to stand clear of her when she got all wound up because she slung a little spit every once in a while and without missing a beat touched the sides of her mouth with a hand-made handkerchief with the initials, DAB, embroidered in curlicues in the corner.

Because she had been to college at some la-tee-dah women's college and to see a couple of Broadway plays, most Mamas who wanted their daughters to be accomplished young ladies regarded Miss Dorothy as the epitome of sophistication and the ultimate arbiter of culture and taste in Brookhaven. Consequently, she made a good living teaching what she called Brookhaven's *crème de la crème* to recite poems like "Ode to a Grecian Urn" with abandonment and affectation. Hard as she tried though her charges didn't learn to speak without a Southern drawl – they just learned to drawl with abandonment and affectation, accompanied by broad, grandly inappropriate gestures.

To help me make the choice between playing the piano and learning to recite "Ode to a Grecian Urn" with abandonment and affectation, Mama took me to one of Miss Dorothy's elocution recitals. I didn't know what to expect. My friend Bird's Mama made him take lessons from her and he tried to tell me what it was like, but that just made it more confusing for me. I couldn't imagine Bird standing still, much less saying poems out loud in front of people.

Miss Dorothy's recital proved to be a wonder to behold. Since her taste in poetry ran toward Romanticism and the classics, she chose passages replete with over-wrought emotions (of love and revenge), obsolete language, and obscure references to mythic knights and princesses. To their credit, Miss Dorothy's pupils really tried to utter their lines with dramatic flair and intensity, but it was also pretty clear from the start that those little girls and occasional odd little boy had no idea what the words they were mouthing meant. As a result, their performances were not unlike what you'd get if you had a bunch of wind-up toys who could recite Byron, Shelley and Keats.

For the finale, all of Miss Dorothy's pupils came out to do a group recitation. It seemed like a good idea, but in reality some of them went too slow, some went too fast, a few went just right and the result was not unlike an elocutionary tug-of-war. Nobody could understand a word they were saying, but appreciated the fact that they were saying it earnestly and enthusiastically. Of course, all their Mamas and Daddies, and a smattering of Miss Dorothy's friends from her First Presbyterian Church Sunday School Class responded with a round of applause. Whether it was a measure of appreciation for the talent of the little elocutionists or an outpouring of relief that it was over and they could go home, I'll never know.

After the recital, Miss Dorothy had a little reception. Quickly spotting Mama and me as "prospects," she came over and kissed up to Mama and talked down to me in that condescending oooshy sweet adult way all children hate. She offered me more cookies and punch, but since the heart shaped puffs had hardly any sugar in them and the punch was a funny color that looked like anti-freeze and tasted like toothpaste, I said, "No, thank you, ma'am" and smiled real big, like I was going to go home and say, "please, Mama, can I take talkin' lessons from Miss Dorothy." But she was wrong. I already knew that my choice wasn't between piano and elocution lessons but between Miss Dorothy and Sister Clare.

Sister Clare won – hands down. Since we didn't own a piano or have any place to put one, Mama arranged for me not only to take lessons from Sister Clare at the convent, but also to practice there. Once, when I was sitting on the piano bench waiting for her, I heard her coming down the steps – fast. When I looked up, she was skipping down the stairs like a little girl. That glimpse of her and the memory of the nuns laughing out loud changed the way I saw nuns forever. But I knew from the git-go that it was going to take more than Sister Clare's charm to make me take to playing the piano.

She tried though. And I tried too. I really did try to get my fingers to arch gracefully over the keys – just so – at the wrists like she wanted me to. I tried to convince myself that practicing scales would some day lead to playing a pretty song, like "You Are My Sunshine" or a classic like the "Blue Danube Waltz." I stuck with it for a year and played "Spring Song" at my first and only piano recital. Great lyrics:

Little breeze from the south,
You can sing though you have no mouth.
Little birds in the trees,
Sing to me their sweet melodies.

After two years in Brookhaven, Sister Clare was shipped out

to another convent. Maybe because she was the first person I ever loved who went away and left me, I really thought my heart would break when she got on a train and left town.

The Illinois-Central Railroad ran right through the heart of downtown Brookhaven on its way from New Orleans to Chicago. The day Sister Clare left town, I went down to the train station with some of her other students to see her off. I wanted to give her a good-bye present, but Mama said nuns didn't have any use for worldly things and she didn't think they were allowed to get presents anyway. I thought about that with mixed feelings. On one hand, it didn't seem fair. Just because she was married to God was no reason not to let her know how much a little girl loved her. On the other hand, I knew Mama was right. I was pretty sure Sister Clare didn't need any Jergen's Lotion or Evening in Paris perfume. I didn't try to give her a good-bye hug, but she held my hand tight and told me to be good girl and got on the train and left. I ran beside the train crying and waving until Mama stopped me and took me home. Then I cried some more.

You would think that Sister Clare's leaving town would be the end of my "Nun Story," but it was really only the beginning. I missed Sister Clare and mourned for her with the intensity of a lonely only child who experienced her first sense of real loss. Her impact on my life was both profound and unforgettable.

Throughout the rest of my childhood and well into my adult life I had a recurring dream. I was in a crowded train station (remember she left on a train), the crowd would part and I would see Sister Clare walking toward me, smiling. She would come close, look me right in the eye and say, "Jimmie, I know everything you have ever done wrong." Then I would stand there stricken by guilt and she would turn and move away and quickly disappear into the crowd again.

Years and years later, I taught 11th grade English in a little town in the middle of a cornfield in Central Illinois. At Christmas that year I rode home on an Illinois Central Railroad train going

South – the same train line Sister Clare had left Brookhaven on – going North.

I sat by a middle-aged lady distinguished by nothing more than an openness that invited conversation. We struck up a conversation, talking about nothing of consequence until it came out that she had a sister who was a nun. You're probably thinking that Sister Clare was her sister. Right? Close. Sister Clare was her cousin. I asked if she knew where Sister Clare was. "No," she said, "I don't know where she is, but my sister is in the same order and I'm sure she can find out." She promised to ask her sister and write and let me know. She took my address.

I got off the train in Brookhaven. She went on to New Orleans, and I never saw her again. I forgot about our chance meeting until one day several months later I got a postcard telling me that Sister Clare was in a convent in Conway, Arkansas.

I labored over the letter I wrote her, beginning rather lamely, "Dear Sister Clare, I know you don't remember me, but…." I then tried to convey to her, without sounding too maudlin, how much she had meant to me and how much she had influenced my life. I told her I was a teacher in large part because of her. I signed the letter – *Jimmie Meese*. I mailed it and waited.   I didn't know whether convent rules back then would allow her to receive a letter, much less write back to anyone not in her family.

But she did write back and I was stunned and reduced to tears by her very first words, "Dear *Jimmie Lonnie*," she began, "of course, I remember you. I've prayed for you every day of your life."

Sister Clare remembered me! Only Mama, Daddy, a few aunts and uncles and some distant cousins and a first grade teacher who had every six weeks written my full name on my report card knew my middle name was *Lonnie*. She not only remembered my middle name, she remembered those angel wings Daddy had so painstakingly engineered. She wrote about how beautiful they were.

I don't know why she remembered me or why it was so important to me to know that she did. I guess not many scrawny little brown-eyed girls had ever gone right up and kissed their favorite nun in class. It was very affirming to know that the nun whose smile and encouragement had meant so much to me, remembered me too and loved me and prayed for me.

And *that* you might think was surely the end of my nun's story, but it was only the middle. I saw Sister Clare three more times after that. On the way to a national debate tournament in Oklahoma, I told my team that I was going to make a detour to Conway, Arkansas and went by and visited her. I found the convent, knocked on the door, and was invited in. I asked to see Sister Clare, not giving my name, only identifying myself as a former student. I heard her footsteps on the stairs, not as fast as when I'd seen her skipping down the stairs for my piano lesson years before, but still briskly. Finally, I was face to face with Sister Clare again. She looked at me, opened her arms, inviting a hug and said my whole name, "Is that really you, Jimmie Lonnie Meese?"

My reunion with Sister Clare lasted less than an hour and when I left Conway, I thought "Okay – now I've seen my nun again. It's closure time." But our paths closed two more times.

Later she was re-assigned to the convent in Brookhaven and in a time of theological indecision I went to talk to her about converting to Catholicism. Aunt Edna who had so feared my being turned into a Catholic years before would have been surprised to know that Sister Clare made no effort to influence me. She just listened and answered my questions and prayed for me.

I saw Sister Clare for the last time just a few years ago. Through a childhood friend who became a nun, I found out that Sister Clare was in a retirement home for nuns in Chattawa, Mississippi. The next time I went to visit my cousins in Wesson I bought some flowers for Sister Clare and went to Chattawa to see her. I arrived unannounced and asked for her, having no idea what she would look like. A pleasant receptionist called her down for a visitor. This time there was no instant recollection. I told her who I was and she thought for a long time and *said* she remembered me, but I don't think she did. Still she knew that she had taught me and was genuinely pleased that I had come to see her. She gave me a tour of the home and we went up to her room and she showed me pictures of her family and gave me a red and white potholder that she had made in retired nuns arts and crafts class. I showed her pictures of my family and told her once again how much she had meant to me. I had my camera and asked someone to take our picture together. My smiling skipping young nun was now short and plump and rosy cheeked. Her hair was straight and white and looked like the oldest May sister might have cut it. Her complexion, pores still never clogged with paint and powder, glowed. No longer in a black and white penguin habit, she was wearing a polyester little-old-lady dress like any grandmother might wear to church on any given Sunday.

I hugged and kissed my kindergarten teacher and loved her every bit as much as I had the day, sixty years before, when I walked up to her desk and surprised her with a kiss.

When I left, she walked with me out to my car and stood there waving as I drove away.

How I Know for Sure Why I'm Afraid of Mice

I suspect everybody has some kind of fear or phobia. I've had my share, and I have no idea where most of them came from. I can't point to a particular convergence or sequence of recurring events that could be pinpointed as causal forces for them. Except for two – my bridge phobia and my rodent phobia.

Repeatedly in very early childhood I had nightmares about being in a car going down a steep hill curving left. All of a sudden, still in the curve, I'd see a bridge at the bottom with low sides and the car would be going too fast to make the curve and would crash through the railing, and I would be in that car falling into a deep ravine with water at the bottom. I'd wake up just before we hit bottom. I'm sure that the reason I have a deeply imbedded fear of big bridges is because of that recurring nightmare. What I'm not sure of is why I had the nightmare.

Was it the symbol of my insecurity born from the unpredictable swings in my parents' moods and behaviors, alternating between double-doting, smothering love that made me the center of their universe or a dream symbol representing my sense of embarrassment and disappointment and insecurity engendered by never knowing when or which one of them would fall off the wagon.

I am sure though that I caught my second full-blown phobia from one of Daddy's aberrant behaviors. The details of the precipitating event are among the most vivid memories I have. Daddy and I were out back of the service station next door to Junior Sartain's Diner. Daddy was checking an inner tube for leaks. He had put air in the tube and was holding it under water and rotating it to see where the air escaped and made little bubbles rise to the surface. The water tank was part of an old hot water heater that had been sliced through with an acetylene torch and set in cement. The water in the tank was never changed, so when it got hot, sludgy dark green algae covered the sides of it. Daddy finished his check, stood up and was wiping the green stuff off on his khaki uniform when W. K. White, one of his fishing buddies, came around the corner of the station holding a dead mouse by the tail.

I don't know where he got it and I think he was just going to chunk it out back some place and had no intention of taunting Daddy, but when Daddy saw W. K. and the dead mouse, he jumped backwards and turned ashy white.

I couldn't believe what I was seeing. My Daddy who in my eyes was absolutely fearless was standing there frozen by fear.

Being something of a natural nuisance and a tease, when W. K saw Daddy's reaction he assumed the swaggering pose of all bullies and started toward him dangling the mouse by the tail and threatening to throw it on Daddy. Big mistake.

As W.K. took a step toward him, Daddy bent down and picked up the tire tool he used to pry off hubcaps. Then he gritted his teeth and through them said to W.K., "W.K., if you come one step closer to me with that thing, I'll kill you, you son-of-a-bitch."

I could tell that he meant it, and W.K. knew it too and backed off.

In that defining moment, I learned two things – my Daddy was not invincible. He had fears. And if the only thing on earth I'd ever seen that could scare my Daddy was a dead mouse – it must be one of the world's most dangerous animals.

That episode ultimately generalized into a full-blown rodent phobia that still makes me jump up on tables and scream at the sight of a mouse just like women in cartoons do. In movies when people open manholes and go down and start slogging through underground sewers and tunnels, I cover my eyes because I know what's coming next and to this day I'm so rodent phobic I am even terrified by the image of a *celluloid* rat.

All God's Creatures — Great and Small

I was an equal opportunity pet chooser. At one time or another I had about every kind of critter that could be tamed and called a pet.

One summer I dug a hole in the ground, put a big galvanized wash tub in it and created "turtle world," a habitat for the half dozen or so turtles that I rounded up that summer when they were trying to cross a road or rummaging under some berry bush. From time to time I rescued an assortment of fragile baby birds that in spite of my efforts to keep them supplied with worms and bugs – usually died anyway.

There was Lady the snow white, blue-eyed cat that slept on a little doll's bed with her own blanket. There were the baby wild rabbits that I found in a hole in the ground in a field that had just been razed by a hay baler. Their nest was filled with, fuzzy down-like fur, shed by their mother to make a safe, soft place for her babies. The produce men at the A & P were so impressed that I was able to keep little wild rabbits alive that they saved me scraps of lettuce and carrots and cabbage and all the other trimmings from the fresh produce department.

I acquired the only pure-blooded dog I ever owned by a form

of adverse possession. A big black lab followed me home from the library one day and gave himself to me. Because he had on a collar and was well-fed, we knew he belonged to someone and Mama and Daddy said I couldn't keep him until we really tried to find his owners. Turned out he belonged to Don Jackson, a boy in my class, whose daddy owned Jackson's Portrait Studio where I had my picture made every year on my birthday.

My Daddy was obsessed with getting an 8 X 10 picture made of me every year *on my birthday* – not the day before or the day after – but *on* my birthday. He had one made of me when I was six weeks old, six months old and every year afterward until he died. Thirty in all. Once during the war when my birthday fell on a Sunday and Daddy couldn't persuade Mr. Jackson to open up and make my picture, he made Mama call a photographer in McComb and paid him extra to open up his studio and take my picture on the Sabbath. I was always embarrassed to bring friends home because of all those 8 X 10 pictures covering the walls in our bedrooms. A veritable Jimmie Lonnie Meese shrine.

Anyway, when we found out his name and who he belonged to, we put Blackie in the car and took him back to the Jacksons. Not long after we got back home, Blackie did too. Back to the Jacksons. Same thing. This went on for a few days. Finally the Jackson's gave up. "He's yours," they conceded.

Turns out Blackie had been some kind of trained guard dog in the war and had been so rigorously trained to sit and stay that once given that command *nothing* could induce him to move before given the release command, "Blackie come." Somehow it didn't work when the Jacksons gave him the command, but when he followed me to a movie, I could say "Blackie sit – stay" and he wouldn't move until I came back out..

Daddy was even more indulgent than Mama was when it came to letting me have critters. Once when we went to Illinois to visit relatives on a farm, I fell in love with some little bitty dwarf chickens – what we called "bantys," and I wanted to take some home with me. Daddy's cousins said I could have all I wanted, and Daddy said I could have all I could catch. He thought that would be a fruitless challenge, but I somehow managed to outrun a half dozen of them and insisted that I be allowed to take them back – to our little garage apartment in the middle of Brookhaven. The whole thing was, of course, utterly impractical, but Daddy, a man of honor who kept his word, granted that since I had caught them fair and square I could take them home. Mama asked a lot of practical questions, but Daddy just ignored her, borrowed a carrying coop from his cousin, tied it on the back bumper of the car and headed back to Mississippi.

Reality set in the minute we hit our driveway. It became obvious – even to me that we could not keep six chickens in a little carrying coop forever. We had to let them out. They were mad, and scared and tired chickens, but when we opened the coop, they did what chickens do. They made a beeline for the biggest patch of grass and bushes they could find in the middle of their new asphalt and cement farm. It just happened to be a half block away in the railroad park across from City Hall.

The appearance of a flock of "banty" chickens in the park evoked considerable interest for awhile. "Where'd the chickens come from?" everybody was asking. I never could bring myself to own up to it and admit that they were mine, though I'm sure the fact that I toted chicken feed up to them every day aroused suspicion. Those chickens scratched and clucked and crowed for a while. In Illinois, they'd learned to stay out of the way of sidestepping cows, tractors, and watchdogs on the farm, but they were totally baffled by the size and sounds of passing trains and cars and apparently too stupid to get out of their way. The flock was quickly wiped out, and with each "accident" my sense of guilt grew. I didn't cry and carry on about them as they bit the dust, because I never figured out how to hug and bond with chickens, but I was really sorry that my insisting on bringing them home led to their early demise.

Then there were the squirrels. One Christmas Daddy got me three little wild squirrels from some pulp-wood hauler. Mama really started pinching her lips and humming when Daddy bought the squirrels. We didn't have a proper cage for them and as soon as he brought them home and set the cardboard box down in the garage apartment, they got out and began terrorizing us, especially my grandmother Meese, whom I called simply "Meese." No Mema or Mamaw or Grandma – just Meese.

She was suffering from some kind of senile dementia – hardening of the arteries or Alzheimer's I suspect, though I don't remember ever hearing a name for what she had. I just knew her mind didn't work right. For several years my Aunts and Uncles and Mama and Daddy took turns having her come stay with them. It was hard for us when it was our turn to take care of Meese because we had so little space. Mama and Daddy were both at the service station pretty much all day long, except on Sundays, and Meese needed to have somebody watching her all the time. Sometimes Ella May looked after her, but a lot of times after school when she was with us that task fell to me.

Most of the time in her mind she was still a young girl and was a pretty good playmate for me, though she would usually stand up late every afternoon, pick up her purse and head for the door saying, "Well, I've got to go home now. Mama needs me." Then I would have to try to talk her into staying a while longer, or bribe her with peppermint candy or as a last resort, put myself between her and the door and block her way. Even with advanced dementia she remained a pacifistic Quaker in her soul and she never tried to push her way through, which was a good thing because I could never have brought myself to tackle my grandmother and hold her down and Mama and Daddy would have never forgiven me if I'd lost her.

Sometimes, Mama and Daddy would let me take her outside. There were three or four huge pecan trees around the apartment and in the fall the ground was covered with the fat fleshy nuts.

Meese loved to help gather them, but because she couldn't see very well and because she tended to topple over when she bent down, I took a little footstool outside and helped her sit down close to the ground Then I'd run off where she couldn't see me and pick up lots of pecans and come back and spread them out on the ground behind her. Then I'd turn her around so she could see them and she'd get all excited about finding so many in one place and while she picked up that pile, I'd go find some more and put them behind her, so she could just keep turning around and around, always finding piles of pecans near her feet.

Once I even took Meese to a Saturday afternoon double feature cowboy movie at the Dixie Theatre. That was the only time I was ever embarrassed by her odd behavior. She had never been inside a movie theatre before and she didn't realize the room was full of other people or that she needed to whisper, so when I led her down the darkened aisle, she kept on saying, "Light the lamp, Ellie, (That was her baby sister's name) I can't see a thing. Won't somebody please get the lamp?" Of course, everybody who heard her and saw me leading her down the aisle started giggling. And that just confused her even more because she couldn't see the people around her in the dark making the sounds.

Anyway, the Christmas Daddy got me the squirrels, Meese was staying with us and when she stayed with us, I gave up my rollaway bed in the dining room and slept on the couch. Because Meese was very old and had arthritis, I'd never seen her move quickly – until the night the squirrels got loose.

The minute those squirrels realized they were free, they started shooting around that little apartment like Roman candles fired off in a box. They climbed up the curtains, leapt from chair to chair, and chased each other around and around the apartment. Given my fear of rodents it was odd that I wasn't scared to death to be in the room with rampaging squirrels. They do look a lot like rats with furry tails, but I thought they were funny. Daddy looked sheepish, realizing how badly he had miscalculated the damage three wild squirrels were capable of doing. Mama just shook her head and pinched her lips even tighter, waiting for Daddy and me to do something, while every time the squirrels made a pass close to Meese she hopped up and did a little jig.

They were way too fast and their teeth were way too sharp to catch barehanded, so Daddy and I had to corner them one by one and throw a rug over them. Then Daddy put his work gloves on, picked them up, put them in a flour sack, and drove them out to Sy Parkman's farm and let them go. Much as I would have loved to be the only kid on the block with three pet squirrels, I knew it was the right thing to do.

The Dog Who Loved Me Too Much

The most faithful four-legged friend I ever had was a mongrel dog that I gave the "high falutin'" name of Patrick Aloysius Snodgrass Higginbotham Meese. *Pat* for short. She was white with liver colored spots shaped like a saddle on her back and one brown ear. Her hair was long and the same texture as a German shepherd's.

I seem to have always had the ability to turn animals into a one-person pet. Pat was never more than a few inches from my feet and was jealous of everything and everybody that competed with her for my attention. She was ferociously protective of me. Mama and Daddy couldn't even raise their voice and fuss at me when she was in the room. When they did, she'd lay back her ears, bare her teeth and crouch down like she was going to spring into attack. But she never actually bit anybody until one day when Bird and Kackie and Ronny and I were playing keep-away in the driveway. We were throwing the ball and running and passing it and yammering and taunting each other the way kids do when they play keep-away.

At one point, I got the ball and tucked it between my arm and my ribs. I started running and Bird started chasing me. Suddenly

41

I stopped and turned around to face him. When I did, he drew back his fist and swung it toward me, aiming for and hitting the ball with a solid "thunk" and dislodging it. Which was what he intended to do.

Unfortunately, all Pat saw was someone aiming a fist at me and all she heard was a blow being landed. She charged at Bird, jumped up on his back, tore his shirt, and left a gash mark right under his shoulder blade. Bird started screaming.

"Jimmie's dog bit me! Jimmie's dog bit me!"

When he calmed down and we looked at his back, it was pretty clear that Pat had *scratched* Bird's back with his claws, not *bitten* him. It didn't matter. Pat was now officially a "bad dog." She'd had her "first free bite" and had to go. Mama and Daddy tried to explain that we just couldn't take a chance that Pat might hurt someone again. Really hurt them. They decided that she would have to be exiled to W.K.White's farm where she could run free and procreate with W. K.'s assorted bird dog, beagle and Callahoola Hawg dawg studs.

I didn't care about her running free and procreating with hound dogs. I didn't want to give my dog away to anybody, to go anywhere, especially since all she was "guilty" of was loving and trying to protect me.

But it was a done deal. When W.K. came to get Pat, we ran away. In the center of our block, behind Uncle Frank's casket warehouse, there was an overgrown lot that apparently was claimed by no one. That's where Ronny and Bird and I had made a hideout. Every kid on the block knew where it was – and no adult did. At the very center of the lot there was a clump of dead shrubs completely covered with honeysuckle and Virginia creeper vines. We'd made a hole in the vines and tunneled into the middle and broken off enough dead limbs in the center to make a dome. Four kids could get in there if we sat on the ground close together. That's where Pat and I headed.

I remember sitting in there hugging Pat and crying and

listening to Mama call me. I knew she knew I could hear her, but I was pretty sure she wouldn't come after us. Even if she did wander into our jungle, she could walk right by us and not see us.

Defiance is an odd emotion, especially in a normally obedient prototypically good child of alcoholics. Logically I knew I'd have to come out and give up my dog – someday. In my heart though I wanted to stay long enough to show them how much I was hurting for having Pat taken away from me – just for loving and protecting me.

Mama pleaded. Cajoled. Threatened. Promised. "You can go see her anytime you want to. You can have one of her puppies."

No deal.

I don't know how long I waited, but eventually I gave up. I came out and W.K. put a rope through Pat's collar and reached out and tried to pat her but she drew back and sulked.

W.K. tried to talk to Pat – sweetly – more to assure me than because he thought she would respond. It was kind of funny actually. Grown men just don't do that well talking sweet to dogs. "Good, doggy, doggy" was about the best he could muster.

I knew W.K. was a good man and I knew he would take good care of her, but when I turned Pat over to him and went inside, I refused to talk to my Mama and when Daddy came home, I gave him the silent treatment too.

They could have made me talk if they'd tried, pulled adult rank and demanded an obedient response, but they didn't. They knew I'd been wronged. They knew taking away a kid's dog, even for cause, was a serious parental offense. So they let me punish them with my silence.

I mourned for my lost dog for a long time and though I finally forgave Mama and Daddy for making me give her away, I never forgot the dog who loved me too much.

The Embalming Room Door

*P*lace shapes you. Where you were born – the country, the state, the side of town, even the house where you were born adds or subtracts from who you are and who you will become. Your language and your culture are, of course, big-ticket items, but in infinite other smaller, more subtle ways, *where you live* molds and makes you who you are. In communication we refer to place as *context;* in argument, as *locus,* but it all means pretty much the same thing. Place shapes you. To a remarkable degree, life is a lot like real estate – it's all about location, location, location.

Take me, for instance. I was born in America, in Mississippi, in a small town, and I always lived in small spaces. I lived in a dark old house near the Illinois Central Railroad track, then in an apartment over the fire station which was behind and attached to the City Library and City Hall. For a while I lived in a tiny one bedroom garage apartment, owned by my Uncle Frank Hartman, the Funeral home and burial insurance king of Brookhaven. There I was pretty much surrounded by reminders of and the accoutrements of death on a daily basis.

Mama and Daddy's bedroom was only large enough for their bed and a dresser. The kitchen had a narrow enameled table and four chairs in the middle of it – and nothing else. Two people could not pass each other in the bathroom. I slept in what would have been the dining room which was only big enough for a roll-away bed and a small book shelf, so the three of us always ate in the kitchen, where we had room for only one guest at a time. The living room was crammed with a sofa, two stuffed chairs, and Mama's favorite possession, a wobbly corner "what not" shelf that she filled with ceramic flowers, perky birds, figurines of bewigged Victorian ladies and men, and some made-in-Japan cigarette and match holders.

Because my room was the converted dining room which was just an opening off the living room, there were no doors that I could close for privacy, though I can't say that privacy was anything I missed or wanted. As an only child, I was alone and lonely a lot and it never occurred to me that I should try to close doors and keep people out.

When we didn't have company, my fold-up rollaway bed was left open. When company came, we closed it up and Mama put a home-made pink flowered slip-cover over it so the room wouldn't be dominated by a folded-up, thin mattress on a wire and metal frame. The only other furniture in my room was a four-shelf bookcase that held my set of World Book Encyclopedias and a burgundy colored plastic record player that Mama and Daddy gave me for Christmas the year they also gave me a burgundy colored imitation leather cardboard suitcase.

When I sat on my bed and looked out the back window, I was staring straight into an always-open doublewide door in the back of the warehouse where burial vaults were stored. Mr. Clay Westerfield and a couple of helpers worked in the service shop in the front part of the warehouse taking care of the fleet of hearses and ambulances that carried the sick, the maimed and the dying to the hospital, and the dead to Uncle Frank's embalming room.

Mrs. Ella Lee's Boarding House sat between our apartment and Uncle Frank and Aunt Belle's house, and it really galled Uncle

Frank that a surly old lady owned a prime piece of property right in the heart of his domain, but Miss Ella was just as hard-headed and stubborn as he was and would never even *talk* to him about selling. Uncle Frank's flower shop was on the other side of his house, next door to his main funeral home building. A labyrinth of walkways, paths, driveways, and alleys dissected that quadrant of the block connecting everything he owned, so Uncle Frank could go from his funeral home to his house to his flower shop to his warehouse and mechanic's shop, to his molasses garage, and his rental duplex and garage apartments without ever having to set foot on a city sidewalk.

Our garage apartment sat behind the duplex that Uncle Frank owned. We had no yard, just a looping arc of a gravel driveway, so my playground and roaming territory was in, and between, and around a real death-business zone.

Sometimes the other kids on the block and I played hide and seek among the big wooden boxes that the vaults came in, and once when I was hiding in one of them with just a little crack so I could look out and breathe, Bird figured out where I was, and to terrorize me, tiptoed up and pushed the lid all the way closed. I was only in total darkness for a split second before I pushed my way out gulping for air in panic, but have had a tinge of claustrophobia ever since and still don't like to be in a room with the door all the way closed.

Another of my funereal pastimes was going to the backroom of the flower shop where the ladies made the wreaths and sprays of carnations and gladiolas for low-end funerals and the blankets of roses to drape over the coffins of the families with money who lived on the west side of the railroad tracks and south of Main Street. When I hung out with those ladies, I pretended that I was a florist too. None of the other kids on the block ever hung out there, but the ladies knew that I was Uncle Frank's wife's cousin's daughter and they let me play in the back and watch them for hours when they weren't too busy with a double-dead-day deadline to meet. When more than one person died at a time, flower orders really poured in and the ladies got a little stressed out. And when there was a full house with bodies in all of Uncle Frank's parlors at the same time, the ladies just looked at me when I stuck my head in the back and shook their heads and I went away. But when they weren't too busy, they would give me pieces of waning, wilting tossed-aside flowers to play florist with. They showed me how to twist wires around stems and when they messed up one of the green paper wrapped straw wreath bases they gave it to me so that I could practice.

One year around Mama's birthday I asked the flower ladies to save me a really big bunch of waning, wilted, tossed-aside flowers so I could make a wreath for Mama. They obliged by tossing aside some puny pink gladiolas, some dried up baby's breath, and a few fern fronds. Then they threw in a few perfectly fresh pink carnations and offered me one of their generic white milk glass bottles that was chipped on the lip.

I said "no thanks" to the vase because I didn't have anything as mundane as sticking stems in a vase in mind for my arrangement. I planned to make a grand wreath for my Mama, so I went out back and plundered around in the trash cans that overflowed with flower shop detritus and pulled out an old straw wreath, plucked some sad rose blooms and wired everything I could find onto the wreath. I decided on an asymmetrical design so I put all the glads on one side, bunched the carnations and the roses all together on the other side, and stuck the baby's breath in around the top. For an added artistic touch, I picked up all the scraps of ribbon I could find on the floor, wrapped a wire around them and tried to tie it all tightly to the bottom of the wreath. Not having completely mastered the secret of tightening wire tautly enough to hold the ribbon against the frame the bow slipped and drooped down a bit sadly off the bottom.

I personally thought it was the most beautiful wreath I had ever seen, but I noticed that when I showed it to the flower ladies, they kept looking at each other as if they knew something I didn't. They apparently thought it odd for a little girl to give her Mama a funeral wreath for a gift. But Mama loved it! Or at least she said she did. You see Mama had a way of paying me compliments that made me feel like I was as swell as Shirley Temple. When Mama said, "Darlin', that's just the most beautiful thing I ever saw in my life," I believed her.

I've tried to think about the most important things my parents did for me or gave me, and the thing I remember most (other than their playing school with me and helping me learn to love learning) was what a "dream enabler" Mama was. I liked to think big and talk big and plan big. I took pipe dreams and pie in the sky to the extreme, and Mama always went along with me. She never ever made me do a reality check or stuck pins in my inflated dreams and schemes.

Once I went out and managed to hang by my legs on a bar on a swing set for a few seconds. I considered it such an amazing feat of skill and bravery that I went home and told Mama that I was a truly gifted acrobat and that I had decided to become a world famous trapeze flyer. Bless her heart, she declared that that would be wonderful and we spent hours after that talking about how famous I would be and how she would design and make costumes for me with lots of sequins and sparklers and beads.

Another of my recurring daydreams was about living out in the country in a big old house with a fenced-in yard where I could have all the pets I wanted. Like Noah planning his ark load, Mama and I would get out the encyclopedia and turn to the page that had the picture of all the breeds of dogs (a page I turned to so often, I can shut my eyes and see those pictures to this day) and we would pick out the ones I would have. Those were Lassie's heydays and my first choice was always a collie followed in no particular order by a cocker spaniel, a St. Bernard, a Great Dane, and a bird dog – for Daddy.

Mama also facilitated one of my other favorite fantasies

– ordering a baby sister from the Sears-Roebuck catalog. For the longest time I thought that was where babies came from, so I pored over the pictures of the little baby models in the baby clothes section. Mama went along with that one for a while too even going so far as to get out the order form and fill it out for me and pretend to mail it.

Well, anyway, when I gave Mama the wreath I made for her and the card I picked out for her all by myself at Woolworth's, I announced that I considered myself such a great florist I thought I'd go to florist school and become a world famous wreath maker. Bless her heart, she looked at that pitiful patched together wreath and declared that she knew I would be a great one because she had personally never seen a more impressive flower arrangement. And we both laughed at the store-bought card I picked out – the one that read "For my Son-in-law."

All in all I had a remarkably sheltered childhood, with no exposure to any *real* danger, but many times, as children are prone to do, I thought I was in a danger zone. Like the night I touched the embalming room door in the dark and saw a ghost.

Though I had seen my Grand Daddy lying in a coffin when I was barely three years old and been to funerals with Mama and cried when they sang "The Old Rugged Cross" and "I Come to the Garden Alone" and passed the open doors of Uncle Frank's wake parlors filled with mourning relatives and seen caskets hoisted up on the shoulders of pallbearers and slid into the back of a hearse, I had never seen a dead body stripped bare and lying on a cold stainless steel table. And I didn't want to either.

At night when there were no wakes at Hartman's Funeral Home, Dewey Jackson walked down the wide hall behind the office and turned out the lights in the viewing rooms, crossed the hall and turned out the lights in the sales room, then walked back down the hall and turned out the lights in the embalming room. When everything in the back was in darkness, Dewey went back to the front office where a single bare-bulb light hung down from the ceiling and sat down to wait for his Daddy.

Dewey's daddy, Old Man Jackson he was called, was Uncle Frank's night watchman. I called Frank Hartman "Uncle" Frank because Mama told me to and she told me to because she and his wife were second cousins. This made no sense to me because I figured if we were cousins, I should call him Cousin Frank, but Mama and Daddy said that would be disrespectful. Since he was "family," I wasn't supposed to call him *Mister* Frank, and, of course, I believed the world as I knew it would have come to an end if I had ever called him just plain *Frank*.

It was hard to figure *what* there was for Old Man Jackson to watch when there was no dead body in the building, or *why* he would need to watch when there was. But he was good at sitting in the office all night and for a man nearing eighty, there wasn't much else he could do in Brookhaven, so it was the perfect job for him.

Dewey and Old Man Jackson passed each other every night, and as near as I could tell, never spoke to each other. Dewey sat in the chair by the desk until his daddy came all the way into the room. They looked at each other, acknowledged each other by nodding slightly and grunting simultaneously, then Dewey stood up, Old Man Jackson sat down, and the changing of the Jackson guard was complete.

The viewing and visitation rooms filled with flower sprays and bouquets were where families sat near coffins and mourned. There was some sort of mourning cast system in Brookhaven that was closely correlated with how much money the family had, which church they belonged to and whether they lived in town or out in the country.

Generally speaking, and of course there were exceptions, but generally speaking country folks moaned and wailed and sometimes went weak in the knees and collapsed under the weight of their raw grief or the bootlegged whiskey they tried to numb it with. Blue-collar town folks cried a lot too, but rarely out loud. And the rich folks, white-collar professionals and, of course, Episcopalians bore their grief silently, solemnly, stoically.

At open casket wakes everyone walked by the coffin, looked down, and always – always said, "don't he look natural?" or "looks just like herself, don't she?" No matter how grotesque the death mask was or how much bright red lipstick one of the old maid May sisters, who operated the May Sisters Modern Beauty Salon, used to paint on one last smile, the comments were always the same, "don't she look natural?"

Sometimes the family didn't open the casket for viewing, which made the mourners feel cheated. Especially the pros. There was a bunch of women in Brookhaven and a few men who lived to go to the funeral home to visit grieving families. If they had even a slight connection or faded memory of the deceased, they dressed up and went to the funeral home to sign the guest book and offer their sympathy. They didn't wait for someone in their own family or their close friends to die, they mourned distant cousins, in-laws, in-laws of in-laws and people they once passed on the street. If they recognized the deceased's name, they dressed up and went to mourn.

I think that part of the reason they felt deprived when the casket was closed was because they used the viewing as a final check to affirm that they had seen the deceased some where before – that the person in the coffin was, in fact, who they thought it was. This was especially important if the deceased were named something common like Smith or Jones. Brookhaven was filled with *Troys and Roys and Bud and Bubba Smiths and Mays and Fays and Sue Joneses.* They were just checking to be sure they had the *right* dead Bud Smith.

I heard Mama and her best friend Irma speculating once on *why* these mourners came so often. One theory was that they had more clothes than they had places to wear them and just liked to get dressed up. There was also some speculation that the women were sex starved and needed to be hugged, so they came to the funeral home where it was acceptable to hug Dewey or Stinky Martin, Uncle Frank's senior hired huggers.

I think they finally concluded that maybe the serial sympathizers were just plain lonely. Or it could have been that they just discovered something they were good at and took the biblical injunction not to hide their light under a basket to heart literally. Their talent was empathetic mourning, so they went to lots of funerals to practice and perfect their art. And they were remarkably adaptive. They moaned with the moaners; cried with the criers, and sat bolt upright in stony silence with the Episcopalians.

If ever there were a room made for silence, it was the sales room. That's where families went to pick out the casket and vault for their loved one. I'm sure Dewey and Stinky weren't vulture-like the way the death salesmen were later depicted in *American Way of Death*, but somehow, subtly, they did usually manage to show the cheap stuff in a way that made families feel guilty if they chose the "bare bones" (so to speak) option.

Choices ranged from barely padded boxes with little bitty pillows to the over-sized, custom-made models built to bury the likes of over-sized women like Aunt Belle. They were plush and "comfortable," adorned with silks and satin and lace and ruffles and pleats.

And then – there was the darkened embalming room. I can't describe the inside of it. I never opened the embalming room door, but outside a stepping stone path that was wedged in between the flower shop and the funeral home passed right under the embalming room window. There was a huge fan in the window. In the daytime in the summer when I passed by and that fan was on, I knew that Dewey and Stinky were in there doing their vampire job. That's what we called the embalming room – the Vampire Room. Putting all logic and reason aside, because I knew that death wasn't really in the air being blown out by that fan and that I couldn't "catch it" like one catches a cold, I still held my breath and walked on the far side of the path as fast as I could to stay as far away as I could from the smell of death when that fan was on.

So, it is all the more remarkable that late summer evenings one of the favorite games for my friends Ronny and Bird and me was playing the game we called "The Embalming Room Door." After dinner at dusk in the summer time when we got tired of filling jars with lightning bugs or waiting for the mosquito spraying truck to drive by so we could run along behind it and play war in the street, we'd sit down on the steps in front of the funeral home office and talk about stuff kids talked about then, like who had the best horse, Gene Autry or Roy Rogers. Roy Rogers. Who were the funniest cartoon characters – the Little Rascals or the Three Stooges? The Rascals. Who would win a fight between Captain Marvel and Superman? We all agreed that would be a tie. Sometimes when we were really being serious, we tried to relate how far away the moon was to some place we'd been. Ronny said that the moon was about a million times farther away than it was to the state Capitol in Jackson, which was fifty-eight miles north of Brookhaven. Bird didn't think it was that far, and I thought it was farther. None of us could imagine that a man would ever walk there.

But mostly we just sat there building up our nerve and waiting to see who would be the first to say, "Let's play embalming room door." Night after night, summer after summer, we played the same game, sneaking in the funeral home in the dark to see if any of us had enough guts to touch the embalming room door.

Old Man Jackson would hear us come in, but pretend not to see us because he knew that part of the challenge of our game was sneaking in like commandos on a raid. We'd crouch down and whisper and pass the inner door to the office, turn the corner and try to adjust our eyes to the darkness of the hall. To the left, the hall led to the wake rooms; to the right the hall ran for about fifteen feet and then dog-legged left, so if you turned right and went straight down the hall you'd run right into the embalming room door.

On a typical try, we'd each put our right hand on the wall and our left hand on the next person's shoulder and begin inching our way toward that door. Then one of us, usually Bird, would lose his nerve and yell and we'd all turn together with a single sudden motion like pigeons in a parking lot. Then we'd run out past the office to safety, letting the door slam behind us. Sometimes when we were running away, we could hear Old Man Jackson laughing and yelling, "seen a ghost – didja?" Even when we got outside we'd keep on running – past the flower shop and Uncle Frank's house and Miss Ella Lee's boarding house, finally stopping at the edge of Matthew Ard's driveway. Then we'd catch our breath, resume our bravado poses and go home, knowing that the next night or the next, we'd try again.

One night when we were sneaking in, we didn't notice that Old Man Jackson wasn't sitting in his usual place. Like always, we crouched, turned down the hallway and lined up Indian style single-file. I was in front. We took a step forward and nobody broke. Then another and another and another. Still nobody broke. We were farther down the hall than we'd ever gotten before. I had my right arm on the wall and since I was in front, I held my left arm stiff out in front of me so I could feel the door when we got to it without running all the way into it. It was pitch dark and still as a tomb. Believe me pitch dark and still are pitch darker and stiller in a funeral home at night than pitch dark and still are any place else. I could hear Ronny or Bird, probably Bird, hyperventilating – but still nobody broke.

When my fingers touched the wall in front of me, I slid my hand down and around until I felt the unmistakable smoothness of a solid, round, cool-to-the-touch brass doorknob. "We're here," I whispered as I realized that we'd never made a plan for what we would do if we actually made it to the door.

Then as we paused in front of the embalming room door,

there was movement behind us and a very faint shaky white light. We froze, still facing the wall. Then we turned and froze again. A ghost had come out of the casket room and was moving very slowly past the wake rooms. It was coming straight toward Ronny and Bird and me, blocking our way to the exit.

Understand, ghosts seemed just as plausible to me then as angels and devils. If the ether was filled with pretty pink flying cherubs that I couldn't see, smell, hear, taste or touch, and if there was a scalding cauldron of fire and brimstone deep down in the center of the earth where dead sinners spent eternity as bright red critters with tails and horns and pitchforks that eluded sensory perceptions, then why shouldn't I believe that funeral homes were inhabited at night by the spirits and souls of the dead.

Besides – Mama and I had almost seen a ghost at the Wesson Hotel the year before. Mama and I had driven ten miles up to Wesson to check out sightings of the Wesson ghost, first to look at a disembodied whitish glowing form which appeared sometimes to flash on and off across the upstairs balcony of the Wesson Hotel when the 9:10 train passed through and then to check out the tombstones at the Beauregard cemetery.

The ghost at the Wesson Hotel was supposed to be that of a man named Dooley, an Illinois Central Railroad man who sometimes spent his layovers off the 9:10 train at the hotel. Word was that Mr. Dooley was smitten with one of the women who cooked at the hotel. Unfortunately, or so the story went, Dooley got killed by a train at the crossing in front of the Hotel on his way to check in and visit the cook. The Wesson ghost was supposed to be a jealous ghost who hovered around the hotel to frighten away suitors for the fetching cook, and hovered over a little stone in the Beauregard cemetery that read simply *Baby Boy Dooley*.

Mama and I got to Wesson a little early and parked across from the hotel and waited for the 9:10 train to come through. It was a good night for ghost viewing. No moon. No extraneous light. 9:10 came and went, but the 9:10 train didn't. No train. No ghost.

My initial curiosity and anticipation soon gave way to a growing sense of apprehension. After all, I was sitting there waiting to see a *ghost*. I was in a danger zone. I was about to ask Mama if she was sure we were far enough away, when we heard the first faint whisper of the whistle of the 9:10 rounding the curve on the tracks under the bridge over old Highway 51. Then the whisper became a hum and then the hum became a roar. All the hairs in the cowlick on the top of my head stood on end and I reached for Mama's hand. The train didn't always stop in Wesson. Only when there was a signal that someone wanted on or off. It didn't stop this time, but it slowed down a lot and as it did so did the clicking of the cross ties rising and falling rhythmically as the wheels passing over them slowed down too.

I made myself look up at the porch, where sure enough a very small, dim whitish light was making flickering alternate patterns of light and shadow on the front of the hotel. The ghost was there – a very small ghost – shaped like a cross between a bowling pin and Casper the Ghost. I really saw it, and Mama did too. But as soon as the train disappeared, the ghost disappeared too. At first I was sure that I had, in fact, really seen a ghost, but when I thought about it some more on the way home, I realized that the flickering light I'd seen was caused by cars of the train passing between some light and the hotel and casting shadows and shapes of light between the spaces of the gothic rails of the banister that ran across the upstairs porch.

This "ghost", however, the one in the funeral home appeared to be a disembodied head floating in the darkness with a grotesque face, mouth open with teeth bared. We were trapped. The embalming room was right behind us, and the ghost was straight ahead coming toward us and I was sure that *this* "thing" coming down the hall was real. It was real and scary and it kept coming straight toward us.

Just before he reached over and turned on the hall light, I realized that the ghost in the funeral home moved with the same wobbly gait as Old Man Jackson; that this ghost, in fact, *was* Old Man Jackson. When he turned the hall light on, Old Man Jackson was standing there holding a little flashlight right under his chin, up-lighting his face in a grotesque and ghostly way.

"Seen a ghost, did'ja?," he said and laughed at us. Laughed! Old Man Jackson apparently thought scaring three little kids half to death in a funeral home at night was funny.

When I got home and told Mama and Daddy, they thought it was funny too. But I was furious. I had a bad temper back then, a really bad temper, and two things that always made me lose it were getting hurt and getting teased.

Old Man Jackson's practical joke and the fact that we got all the way to the door that night put an end to our game. We never played the embalming room door game again.

But night after night after that when we got tired of catching fireflies and chasing the mosquito spraying truck and debating about Roy Roger's horse, we'd brag about the time we made it all the way to the door of the embalming room and saw a ghost. Over time in the re-telling of our adventure, we became braver and braver and ever more heroic.

Miss Meese Meets Miss Manners

*T*hough Mama's second cousin, Bertha Belle Crawford, had country roots just like Mama, she managed to marry Frank Hartman, a man from Brookhaven who'd never worked in a field or picked cotton, a man with the softest, whitest hands she'd ever seen.

According to her friend, Minnie Maude, Bertha Belle "was just an itty bitty short thang that didn't weigh much more than a hank of hair" when she met Frank Hartman. As Minnie Maude would say, "I don't care if she is my friend, it's the gospel truth that she was the prettiest girl you could ever imagine. She could easy have gone to Hollywood, you know, and made movies with Don Ameche. And I'll tell you somethin' else, Hon, as soon as Frank Hartman set eyes on her, he was a goner."

Every time she said something like that in front of her husband, Buddy, he'd shoot right back at her with, "Well, hell, Minnie Maude, who cares what Bertha Belle looked like in high school. She looks jist like an old sittin' Buddha now."

And she did. If ever a couple's nadir and zenith passed each other on divergent ascending and descending paths – it was Frank and Bertha's. While Frank went from undertaker to bank president, Bertha Belle went from beauty to Buddha. They never had children.

Frank Hartman proved himself to be as shrewd and cunning a businessman as ever earned a dime in Brookhaven. With no actuarial charts to affirm the soundness of the idea, but with enough guts to try it anyway, he started selling burial insurance. For a few dollars a month, he guaranteed to put you or your loved ones in a box in the ground. For an extra dollar or two a month, he'd put the box in a vault before he put the box in the ground, and for various other add-on dollars, you could get a deluxe package that took care of everything from providing flower blankets for the casket to using his newest, finest, longest hearse for the procession through town to the cemetery.

In just a couple of years, he signed up just about everybody in Brookhaven who figured on dying and had an extra dollar a month to spare. His pay-now-die-later plan set Uncle Frank on the way to making his first million dollars.

I never knew whether he bought or built Hartman's Funeral Home, but by the time Mama and Daddy rented one of his little one-bedroom garage apartments, he owned everything from a fleet of hearses and ambulances to a garage full of one gallon cans of homemade sugar cane molasses that he let farmers pay their burial insurance with when they didn't have cash.

While Uncle Frank's wealth increased, so did Aunt Belle. Their combined weight was probably close to 600 pounds. Uncle Frank, who got out and strutted around town in a blue and white seersucker suit with suspenders, was what you would call *portly*. Aunt Belle was what today we would call "morbidly obese." By the time I knew her, Miss Bertha Belle Crawford Hartman's beauty was a thing of the past. Depending on how you define the word *chin*, she either had lots of them – or none at all. Her face began at her hairline and just below her mouth melted into plush layers of over-lapping flesh.

Because she was Mama's cousin, and because she had no

children, and because she had no friends like Mama's canasta and gossip box friends to call and or drop by and chat, Mama felt sorry for her. She didn't feel sorry enough to go visit her herself, but she felt sorry enough to send me over every week or so to keep Aunt Belle company.

"When was the last time you went to see Aunt Belle?" she'd ask.

"I don't know."

"Have you been this week?"

"I don't remember."

"Honey, you know she sits over there by herself all day long, and doesn't have a soul to talk to. It won't hurt you to run over there for a few minutes and talk to her and scramble her some eggs.

That was the oddest part about visiting Aunt Belle. Mama knew I couldn't cook. She never even let me in the garage apartment kitchen when she was cooking. Said it made her nervous. Mama's catch-all excuse/reason for anything she didn't want me to do was to warn me that it made her nervous. Since "nervous" was something I really didn't want to make my Mama, that was all she had to say. I was pretty sure that getting nervous was one of the things that made Mama hum mournful hymns.

I never ever saw Aunt Belle actually stand up and put her weight on her feet. All I ever saw her do was sit in a big old rocking chair when she was well and lie in a big old bed when she was sick, propped up on a pile of pillows with the prettiest pillowcases I'd ever seen. Mama made pretty pillowcases for us with lots of brightly colored embroidered flowers on them that looked cheerful and home-made. Aunt Belle's were hand-made and embroidered too, but hers were all the same color, cream colored thread and lace on cream colored cloth, and hers looked rich and store-bought. I believe my noticing the difference between Aunt Belle's pillowcases and ours was the first time I ever had an inkling about qualitative differences. Our pillowcases were what you called *home-made*. Hers were what you called *hand-made*.

Since I never in the dozens and dozens of times I went to see her, ever saw her stand up, put her three hundred plus pounds on her itty bitty feet and walk, I still don't know for sure how Aunt Belle got from one place to another. Because she couldn't do anything for herself, Uncle Frank hired Bessie, his personal driver Leander's wife, to come clean up and cook Aunt Belle's breakfast and dinner and leave something around for supper. But sometimes she got hungry after Bessie went home.

The first time Aunt Belle asked me to go in the kitchen and scramble her some eggs I just stared at her. She repeated her command as if she thought I hadn't heard it the first time. She tried to make it sound like a request, but we were both aware that she was married to the richest man in Brookhaven and Mama and Daddy and I lived in a little box that her husband owned. I still didn't say anything. I wasn't trying to be disrespectful. The problem was I couldn't say "no" to Aunt Belle, but I also couldn't bring myself to say, "I don't know how." Correctly concluding that my inertia was rooted in ignorance, not defiance, she prodded me more gently.

"Go on in the kitchen, child, and I'll tell you what to do."

"Yes, ma'am."

She walked me through it.

"Get the little skillet that's under the oven."

"Yes, ma'am.

I found it.

"Put some butter in it."

I did.

"Get a mixing bowl out of the cabinet by the sink."

"O.K."

"What – did – you – just say to me? She drew the words out – icily.

And I froze.

"Yes, ma'am," I said quickly, realizing she had picked up on my disrespectful "O.K." response.

"Now get some eggs."

"How many?"

"Two. No – three – no – make it four."

The first eggs I "fixed" for her must have been all right because just about every time I visited her after that we had a little routine. I scrambled four eggs for her, sat down and watched her eat them and waited quietly until she delicately touched her handkerchief to her lips and proceeded to give me a manners lesson.

Mama and Daddy had no pretensions about being "genteel." After their one time shot at making me an accomplished young lady via piano or elocution lessons, they gave up on trying to school me in the social graces of the times. (I was thus spared the humiliation of trying to learn to tap dance or twirl a baton.) Their manners customs were pretty simple. Mama demanded of me that I invariably follow *yes* and *no* with *sir* or *ma'am*. She constantly reminded me to sit up straight and hold my shoulders back, and she always nailed me when I made an "ih" for "eh" substitution and said *git* instead of *get*. And she always made me wear gloves to church, or at least "tote" them with me. That was about all the Emily Post stuff she knew.

Aunt Belle, on the other hand, in spite of the roots and bloodlines she shared with Mama considered herself, purely by virtue of Uncle Frank's position, one of Brookhaven's social elite. Because she had no children of her own to "raise right" and because Mama was, after all, her second cousin, she felt obligated to spend at least part of each of our visits playing Henry Higgins to my Eliza Doolittle.

She spent one whole visit talking to me about forks and spoons and where you were supposed to put them on the table. I thought she was being more than usually obsessive when she started talking about setting a table because I couldn't imagine why on earth one would need more than one fork or spoon or why it mattered where you put it – as long as you could reach it.

She also tried to give me advice on how to cross my legs like a lady, but, bless her heart, because her own legs were so short and fat it was impossible for her to demonstrate.

I was fundamentally a very polite child and tried to feign interest in lessons on leg-crossing, table utensils and how to sit down in and get up out of a chair. I told Mama about our lessons and asked her why Aunt Belle or anyone else would need to be taught such things. She said it was because Aunt Belle tried to act refined, but that explanation was in itself confusing since the only other context I knew for the word *refined* was in reference to sugar and I wasn't sure what that meant either.

Usually after Aunt Belle finished her eggs and my "etiquette lessons," she'd motion for me to sit in Uncle Frank's rocking chair across from her so she could watch and test me. I'd try my best to sit down "like a lady" and cross my legs at the ankles and fold my hands in my lap and sit still "like a lady," but the real me would soon start wiggling and fidgeting and scratching. I was usually barefooted. I always had scabs on my knees and elbows that itched and I never met a scab that didn't need picking at. There was always dirt under my fingernails.

At that age, my single redeeming feature, and the only thing about myself that I ever really liked were my big brown eyes. Grown-ups were always saying I looked smart – or old – or wise. I think I just unnerved them because of my habit of looking everybody right straight in the eye. Very solemnly.

So Bertha Belle Crawford Hartman and I, this fat old Buddha beauty and this scrawny little tomboy, would just sit there and stare at each other. She would rock and stare at me, and I would rock and stare back at her. In silence. Then the Miss Manners thing would start up again. Sometimes she'd have a theme or a topic that she would talk about like a teacher. Other times she'd just stare at me until I did something wrong so she could correct me.

I could always set her off by either moving my right index finger close to my nose or by making a sucking sound that she hated. I didn't really pick my nose that much, but if I so much as moved my finger close to my nose, she gasped and chided me.

"Young ladies do not – simply do not pick their noses."

Her use of the plural *noses* created an image that made me want to laugh, but I just said:

"Yes, ma'am, I know."

Then we'd rock some more, and then I'd curl my tongue up over my top front teeth and pull it back in while inhaling. This produced a sound that I cannot write with letters of the alphabet. It was something like *tcchhh* followed by *sshcblup!* And it drove Aunt Belle crazy.

"Jimmie Lonnie Meese!" She didn't ever raise her voice, but she mustered a whole lot of intensity when she called me by my full name.

"Ma'am?"

"Why *do* you make that awful sound?"

"I don't know, Aunt Belle."

"How many times have I told you – young ladies do not suck their teeth."

"I don't know how many times you've told me," I said, giving her a literal and direct answer which seemed to annoy her even more because she had intended it as a rhetorical question.

"Let me tell you something, Miss Jimmie Lonnie."

That was another thing she did. When she really wanted to convey her distaste, she'd add *Miss* to my name. If she could have walked on those little tiny feet of hers, I think she would have come over and shook her fat little finger in my face.

"If you keep on picking your nose and sucking your teeth and sitting all hunched over, you will never grow up to marry a well-off man – like I did." She usually punctuated our sessions with a pained look and a long deep sigh of resignation and futility.

"I'm sorry, Aunt Belle, I'll try to do better."

That's what I *said*, but what I *thought* was, why on earth would I want to get married and spend my life like the beautiful Bertha Belle – sitting in a big old rocking chair depending on her second cousin's daughter to scramble her some eggs?

Damn It, Daddy, It Got Away!

*L*ike place, *first* things have special significance in one's life and slip right into long term memory with ease and stay there. Children, even very young children, seem to sense this and seek out and note and celebrate firsts in a special, joyful way. There are, of course, classic, and I suspect virtually universal firsts, most of which center on romance in some form or other – first dance, first date, first kiss. But each of us also has a storehouse of memories of special *firsts* that are just ours.

My special firsts were an odd lot of disparate things: the first Indian head penny that turned up in the cash register drawer at Daddy's service station – the first fossil rock I found in some gravel out in front of Uncle Bud's house with a fern imprint – the first conch shell I held to my ear that still had some sand and the distant roar of the ocean in it.

But my all time favorite was the day I went worm-digging and fishing with my Daddy for the first time.

One morning Daddy waked me up early and said we were going to drive out to Silver Creek, a two-hops-and-a-jump-wide little creek half way between Brookhaven and Monticello. I didn't even think about asking why. I did a lot of things with just Mama and me, but going off alone with Daddy was a new experience in itself.

When we got to the creek, he pulled off the road and stopped in the shade of a big old sweet gum tree. Then he took a shovel out of the trunk of the car and motioned for me to follow him.

There was a feeling and a smell about little creeks and branches back then that I can't begin to describe, but remember vividly to this day. Unpolluted creeks, like most of the little creeks in Mississippi still were in the 40s, smelled fresh and clean. Not fresh and clean like perfumed laundry fabric softener – not fresh and clean like Mama's talcum powder, but naturally sweet and fresh and clean – like a baby puppy's breath or grass that has just been mowed. And there was a coolness under the shade canopy by a creek in motion that felt every bit as good as it did standing in front of the icebox with the door open in July – something I was always doing and something Mama was always telling me not to do.

It was that day with Daddy that I first fell in love with the smell and feel of creeks and the touch of wiggling worms. Forget those *Sound of Music*, Julie Andrew's favorite things like *rosebuds* and *whiskers on kittens*. That day I discovered that one of my favorite things was picking up worms while Daddy turned over shovelfuls of dark moist creek bank dirt.

Soon after that, I learned that I loved, not just worm-digging, but all forms of fish- bait-getting: seining shallow creeks for little darting minnows, scooping up crawdads with a long handled net as they scooted backwards and tried to burrow in the mud, and tickling catalpa worms to make them loosen their grip and fall off catalpa trees. Finding fish bait was like an Easter Egg Hunt to me. Each involved searching for something you couldn't see and each discovery was followed by an almost primal rush of adrenaline.

When Daddy turned over a shovel full of creek bank dirt and red wiggling worms started trying to suck themselves back into their holes, my job was to grab them fast and put them in a coffee can. If they got all the way back into their holes, my job was to break up the clod on a search-and-secure mission trying not to tear the worm apart in the process.

I know the very word *worm* makes some people queasy, but I really liked touching worms. Especially catalpa worms. They were fat and yellow and black and beautiful and soft and velvety to the touch. It didn't matter that they stained your fingers when they spit out dark green chewed-up-leaf-juice or left a pile of little green poop pellets in your hand or tried in vain to punish you with their itty bitty pinchers. They made great bait for bottom-feeding mud cats, the cross-eyed prehistoric looking creatures that fought like little sharks. Getting a catfish off the hook was always a challenge because they were so feisty and they always carried their fight out of the water and kept on sparring using their fins to inflict as much pain as possible to the hands of their captors.

I also loved going after crawdads with Daddy, scooping them up out of mud holes under bridges in the hot part of summer when little creeks all but dried up and left smaller and smaller puddles of water and larger and larger islands of parched, cracked dry creek bed bottoms exposed to the sun.

When I got a little bit bigger, Daddy started letting me help him seine for minnows. He rigged up a home-made seine by stringing a piece of netting between two poles and putting some heavy washers on the bottom to keep it weighted down. My job was to stand in the shallow water of a creek, hold one pole pretty much in place and swivel on my axis while Daddy walked in an arc with the other pole, dragging the bottom of the net along the bottom of the creek.

My excitement peaked when he completed the arc and got his pole back to the bank. I always hoped that we'd pull up a grand-daddy catfish or a displaced bass or, at worst, that the net would be absolutely full of red-bellied sun perch and goggle-eyes. More often though, the seine was just full of bottom debris, and if we were lucky, a few flippin'and floppin' bait minnows.

That day Daddy brought two thin dried bamboo poles. He'd cut one of them down to a manageable length for me and rigged both with a cork (back then bobbers were actually made out of natural cork), a hook, and a lead sinker.

When I got a little older, we'd walk a mile or two up and down creeks looking for "honey holes," but that day we stayed close to the car and fished almost under the low-sided bridge, ducking when passing cars slung loose gravel over the edge. A little sand bar island divided the stream there and the whole thing wasn't more than eight or nine feet wide. Daddy took off his shoes, rolled up his pants legs, picked me up, stepped down into the knee-deep water, put me on the sand bar, baited my hook, plopped it in the water next to a log sticking out from the other bank and handed the pole to me.

You know, luck has a lot to do with how you live your life and spend your days. If the fish hadn't been biting that day, if I'd stood there holding that stick in the water for an hour or so with nothing happening, I might have one day become obsessed with some other hobby – canoeing or magic or juggling – but the fish *were* biting that day. When the bobber hit the water, it wobbled on the surface for a split second and then something yanked it straight down and out of sight. I was so surprised by the disappearance of my cork that I just stood there and stared at the circles moving out from where the cork had been. To his credit, Daddy resisted the urge to grab the pole and catch the fish for me. He just stood beside me and kept saying "you've got a fish on your line – pull, pull, pull!"

I did pull, and when I did, something alive pulled back. If you've never hooked a fat little ole bright red and yellow sun perch, you can't believe how hard those little boogers can pull. I pulled back on that line with all my four-year-old might and the something still unseen under the water pulled back harder.

This is one of those things that if you don't get it, I probably can't explain it to you, but there is a moment when a fish is on the line and you still can't see it because it hasn't broken the surface of the water yet that *anticipation* and *hope* are distilled and pure. Though I surely couldn't conceptualize it then, that was the moment I first learned that *anticipation* of something good – *anticipation* of something exciting is one of the strongest motivating forces in life.

I would later experience the same feeling at the finish line at a racetrack when I bet on a horse that made it to the finish line running neck and neck for the lead and when I pulled the handle of a slot machine and watched the drums spin around and land on three golden bells in a row.

All I know is that as soon as that first little perch came out of the water, I realized that it had hooked me as hard or harder than I had hooked it and I've had an obsessive addiction to fishing ever since.

I've thought about it a lot and decided that another reason I love fishing as much as I do is because the best times I ever spent with Mama and Daddy were spent *on* or *by* or *in* water – fishing together. It was the only thing we did all together for fun. And oddly enough, when they were fishing neither of them drank. It was as if the hypnotic repetitiveness of fishing was so soothing, they needed nothing else to bolster them. In my favorite picture of Mama and Daddy and me, I was about three years old and we were by a river. I was in my bathing suit with a silly rubber swim cap on. Mama and Daddy were sitting side by side. Daddy had on a dress shirt and tie and had his pants legs rolled up and his bare feet in the water and he was holding a cane fishing pole. Mama sat close to him and had on a dress-up dress that she was holding in around her legs demurely. I don't remember the day at all and can't imagine why Mama and Daddy were all dressed up to go to the river. But I love the picture.

On the Fourth of July we used to take a watermelon and fried chicken and pimento cheese sandwiches and spend the day by the little creek that ran through Horace and Hattie Cato's pasture. They were good customers of Daddy's and didn't care if we went on their land. Some people believed that Hattie was the *unluckiest* woman alive and just as many thought she was the *luckiest*. The opposing conclusions were based on the same events. She was the only woman in Lincoln county to have survived being bitten on the butt by a black widow spider while sitting in her outhouse *and* to have survived touching a high power electric line while trying to keep their cows from getting fried by a downed power line in their pasture.

Anyway, we'd put the watermelon in the creek when we got there to get it cooled by the water flowing over the sandy bottom. Lots of times Ella May would go with us too, and sometimes we'd take a skillet and some Wesson oil and corn meal and Daddy would clean the fish we caught, build a fire and Ella May would fry the fish and we'd sit there and eat the crispy little perch, tail and all, and then lie on a quilt and take a nap.

During the war, Daddy got a job as a fireman and we moved into an apartment over the fire station. All the old men who gathered there to play cards and checkers and brag were seasoned fishermen. They told Daddy about going fishing in the swampy low lands in Louisiana on the other side of the Mississippi River. While the Mississippi side of the river was mostly bounded by high bluffs, the Louisiana side was flat and pocked with bar pits made when crews dug out dirt to mound up for the miles of levee that were built to hold back "Old Man River" but which every decade or so were breached by the flood tides of melting snow from the North. There were also dozens of horseshoe shaped lakes along the river. They were formed when for some reason over time, the river changed course, carved out a new channel, changed course again and left distinctive arc-shaped lakes behind. They were like huge fish bowls being filled and refilled with fish every time the river overflowed and receded again.

Daddy first went to Louisiana on a *serious* fishing trip with Red Myers and some other old men from the fire station. Then after he learned the ropes, he started taking me with him. Just Daddy and me. He bought a little two-or-three-horsepower Johnson outboard motor, which compared with the giants they put on the back of boats now, looked more like an egg-beater than an outboard motor.

Those trips to the bayous began in the middle of one night and ended in the middle of the next and were absolutely grueling. According to Daddy, we had to be at the fishing place at daybreak or it wasn't worth the drive, so we left Brookhaven at midnight and drove to the ice house in Natchez. There a huge black man took ice tongs, disappeared into the coldness and came back with big blocks of ice for the galvanized tubs we took with us to haul our catch home. Then, because of my bridge phobia, I lay down on the seat and hid my eyes as we crossed the Mississippi River Bridge in darkness and stopped in Faraday, Louisiana, to buy minnows from a shoeless old Cajun whose feet fascinated me because I had never seen anything else so dirty in all my life.

Years and years later, I took a graduate course in Intellectual History and wrote a paper de-romanticizing some of the natural-man myths about the Cajun culture. Back then, I just loved listening to the lilt in the old Cajun's speech and the primitive beauty of their shacks and sagging, leaning piers that we passed on the long ride down the Bayou.

About fifteen miles west of Faraday we turned left, went south a few miles and turned left again toward the lakes and bayous that lay beside the ever-moving-on Mississippi River. We went from narrow two-lane roads to even narrower ones; from gravel roads to mud roads and finally to plank roads.

One night, when we came to a little low-sided one-lane bridge, Daddy stomped the brakes. I was half-asleep, but popped up to see why we stopped. We were in the middle of the bridge surrounded by a herd of goats. Daddy expected the goats to get out of his way. But they didn't. They just stood there staring into the headlights. Daddy, not a patient man on his best days, was in a race with sunrise and wasn't about to sit back and wait until a bunch of goats yielded the right-of-way. He started honking the horn and revving the engine to make noise and started moving forward slowly toward the goats. When the front bumper slowly touched the first goat, all hell broke loose. That goat stood on its hind legs like it was going to attack the car. When it did that, all the other goats started bleating and bucking and butting each other and jumping over the sides of the bridge like lemmings.

When the road cleared, Daddy took off again. I looked back at the empty bridge and couldn't help asking him, "Daddy, do you think there was any water under that bridge?"

Coming back that way later that day, I dreaded crossing the bridge again. I half expected to see a pile of broken goats on either side, but there wasn't a goat in sight, so I asked Daddy if he thought goats, like cats, always landed on their feet. Mama always tried to answer my questions, even when she didn't know the answer. Daddy in true Meese-man fashion only responded when he knew the answer. That day he didn't answer me, but I could tell he wondered too.

Anyway, when we got to the boat landing, Daddy woke up one of the Boudreaux children to rent a boat. When we came back in the afternoon, Pappy Boudreaux would be there, offering the services of his children to "gut and gill" our catch, but in the morning it was always one of the sleepy Boudreaux boys who stumbled out, unlocked the chained boat and gave us a paddle in case our motor died.

All the Boudreaux children were scrawny and didn't look like they ever got enough to eat. Everyone of them had skinny, skinny little chicken necks, lots of scabs and bug bites, and red rimmed eyelids covered with the crusty stuff that gets in the corners of eyes when you're asleep. They were browned from the sun and none of them wore shirts – not even the girls until they started growing little breast blossoms. But you could tell that they were tough and feisty kids. When we came back to the landing, they were everywhere – swimming, water fighting, diving, fishing, cleaning fish, chasing their raggedy dogs, all the while whooping and hollering. They jabbered to each other all the time with their sweet Cajun tones and cadences, but never said anything to Daddy and me except "Yes, sir" and "Nome." Even the ones who were older than me used the Southern polite form of address when speaking to me, reducing "no ma'am" simply to *"nome."* For the most part they studiedly ignored us, as if they not only represented another strain of culture, but as if they lived in an enclosure in another world. But they were little fishermen to their toes and like all fishermen every where could never resist running over to check out our catch.

In those days we didn't have a fancy insulated cooler. We just took an old galvanized wash tub to haul home our catch, and when it was too heavy for Daddy to tote up the steep bank, Pappy would nod and one of the boys would come take hold of a handle and help Daddy carry it. Pappy invariably asked Daddy if we wanted his boys to "gut and gill" our fish because they made good tips that way, but Daddy always said *no* and we took our catch home and sat out in the back yard and cleaned them ourselves.

When Daddy got the boat loaded, we'd head off, still in the darkness to a lake eight or ten miles deep into the bayou. I'd sit in the front of the boat shining a flashlight ahead of us to be sure we didn't hit a submerged log or sunken boat and shear a pin on the motor. I never really understood why we had to go so far down the bayou before we started fishing when every single place we passed looked fishy to me – especially compared to the little shallow creeks and muddy farm ponds we fished in at home.

Everyone has special sensory memories of sights and sounds and tantalizing smells from childhood. Some more vivid than others. The most spectacular sight memory I have is of sunrise on Cocodrie Bayou. When the sun crept up over the cypress trees laced with Spanish moss, pinks and oranges and lavenders slid across the sky and everything woke up. As we moved though the darkness, the flashlight beams would catch the yellow eyes of all kinds of critters in and around the bank, wedged between the cypress knees and the fallen trees and sagging piers. At daybreak we could begin to see the critters that belonged to the eyes.

There wasn't a lot of noise. A bullfrog whonked from time to time. Sometimes an owl screamed at us, and every once in a while a great blue heron squawked about our coming through and messing up its fishing hole. One of the sweetest sounds I've ever heard came from a v-shaped flock of geese that flew honking in, circled around just over our heads and landed in front of us. All those wings putting on brakes at the same time made the most wonderful sound – a whirring *whooosh* sound – like a cross between a whisper and the wind.

Unlike the birds, all the land critters managed to move in an eerily silent way. They slid and slithered and snuck and skulked out of sight.

Then Daddy would spot the landmark he was looking for and make the pronouncement I was waiting for. "This is the place," he'd say. Then he'd cut off the motor, get out his paddle and we'd bait up and start fishing.. I don't think we ever went into that swamp and came back empty handed. Once we almost filled a galvanized wash tub with bream, which is mostly what we caught, though what made fishing in the bayou so much more exciting than creek fishing at home was knowing that at any minute your cork could go under and you'd pull back and you'd have something so big on the line that it would feel like a refrigerator.

There was always a chance there that you'd get one of those variable ratio payoffs and catch a really big catfish or bass or grinnell or – the dreaded trash fish – the gar! Daddy hated gars. He'd cut his line rather than pull one into the boat. While I pretended to share Daddy's contempt for gar, I always secretly hoped I'd hang one. To me *a fish was a fish was a fish* and anything on the end of the line was better than nothing on the end of the line, so sometimes when I saw a gar circling near the surface, I'd deliberately throw my bait close to it, hoping to induce a bite and a fight.

While our best trips were the ones to the swamps and bayous of Louisiana, all fishing trips were special. Daddy and I and sometimes Mama fished in creeks, ponds, lakes, rivers and the Gulf of Mexico. We caught bream and bass and catfish and crappie and grinnel and gar in fresh water and speckled trout, flounder, sheep head and Spanish mackerel in the Gulf of Mexico. I can't begin to describe every trip and every fish I caught, but to this day I can close my eyes and see in vivid detail hundreds of places I have fished and *every* place I've had a run in with a snake.

If you spend enough time walking trails along creek banks in Mississippi or spend enough time sliding under thick branches and vines over-hanging water, you *will* have a run-in with a snake. In the course of my hundreds of fishing adventures, I met more than one water snake up close and personal.

The first one. When I was seven or eight years old I was fishing alone in Uncle Bud's farm pond in the back pasture. The pond wasn't a whole lot bigger than a bathtub. The dam was ringed with high weeds and little pond willows. The water was ochre colored, perpetually Mississippi-mud-muddy and murky from Uncle Bud's milk cows wading into the middle to cool off and try to escape the gnats and skeeters and flies that hung over them no matter how fast or hard they flicked their tails.

But to me water was water. A pond was a pond, and I was determined to fish. I took the old cane pole Uncle Bud kept for me out behind the smokehouse, went out in the cow pen, flipped over a few cured cow patties and pulled out some fat squirmy worms. I followed the path to the pond that the cows and unchecked rain water had worn down between the scrub oaks and underbrush. I fished for a while and got a few nibbles and caught a few pale stunted bream. It really didn't matter whether I was catching a lot of fish or not. You see, if you really like to fish, it's the *fishing* itself that matters. *Catching* is an added bonus but it's the fishing that matters.

After a while, my cork twitched again, stopped, then twitched again and slid slowly and decisively under the surface. It was an odd bite. Bream didn't pull that slowly and the little ones in this mud-hole weren't big enough to pull it down so far. Could be a turtle. Or a BIG fish, though that seemed unlikely. I held my breath and pulled back slowly. Strong resistance. Something writhed on the other end of the line.

Even at that age, I was attuned to the characteristic motions of various fish. Bream attacked and darted. Bass either exploded on the bait or fiddled with it. I tried to visualize what a bass looked like under water, nudging the bait with its nose or whatever the thing that fish have between their eyes is called, then slowly picking up the bait and swimming away, pulling the bobber sideways and under. Turtles pulled bait one way, catfish another, but nothing I had ever had on a line pulled the way this *something* was pulling – with a slow rotating motion.

I kept on pulling until finally a head emerged, a head somewhat like a turtle head but with a long neck – a very, very long neck. In fact, it was all one long skinny neck I kept thinking until it finally registered that it wasn't a turtle at all! Hook firmly embedded in its mouth, there was a snake writhing on the end of my line! I couldn't tell what kind it was, but I assumed that because it was a snake and because it was in the water, it was a water moccasin. I could tell for sure that whatever kind of snake it was, it was a very, very angry snake. And I was sure that it was as startled to get yanked out of the pond as I was to be doing the yanking.

I'm also pretty sure I screamed. I know absolutely positively for sure that I hurled the pole, hook, line, cork, weight and snake into the water and started running as fast as I could back to Uncle

Bud's house. At a considerable and what I considered to be a safe distance, I tuned back to look at the pond, half expecting that snake to be pulling that pole right behind me, but the pole was still floating in the pond, moving very slowly toward the dam.

I went to Uncle Bud's dozens of times after that, and I fished in his other pond, but I never went back to that mud hole in the back pasture again, forever harboring the irrational fear that if I went back I'd still see that fishing pole being pulled slowly around and around the pond.

That was the first, but not the last snake I ever caught or had an otherwise close encounter with.

One of Mama's friends, Miss Nellie Smith, had a lake that had more bass in it than any other place I fished around home. And more snakes. Mama was scared to go there because of all the snakes, but by the time I was in my teens and could drive the car and go fishing by myself, I felt pretty invincible and went to the snake lake a lot.

The snakes there were so bold that when I put my stringer of fish in the water at my feet, snakes would swim right up and try to eat them off my stringer. Turtles were always bad to do that, but Miss Nellie's was the only place I ever fished where the snakes were that bold.

One day I was sitting on a little point that jutted out into the lake when I saw a big snake coming straight after my fish. He was so big and swimming so purposefully, I picked up the stringer and never taking my eyes off the snake started pulling the fish out of the water and dragging them along the ground as I walked backwards up the bank. That usually stopped them, but this snake slithered out of the water and kept on coming, following me and the fish. I probably should have just dropped the stringer and let it have them. But they were my fish, I caught them and the snake had made me mad. At the top of the bank, I stopped backing up and turned and headed back to the car. Not as fast as if there were a mouse behind me – but fast.

I've always been very clear about the difference between phobias and plain old fears. Ever since I saw Daddy threaten to kill his friend, W. K. White, for taunting him with a dead mouse, I have been phobic about rodents, irrationally afraid of mice, but I was only rationally afraid of snakes. I was cautious around them, but not screaming, hysterically afraid of them, so instead of vowing to stay away from Miss Nellie's pond like Mama did, I went back to the very same spot the next day, but I took Daddy's pistol with me, armed to do battle with that snake if he came at me and my fish again. And come he did! No sooner than I caught a fish and put it on a stringer, tossed it back in the water and stuck the end in the bank, I saw him swimming straight toward the point. Again he swam purposefully, not warily like most snakes moved. He was an arrogant snake.

When he got close enough, I dropped a minnow right in front of him and as the lead weight pulled the minnow down, the snake slid his head under the water and headed straight after my minnow. The cork went under. I gave the line a little slack and then pulled back. Unlike the time at Uncle Bud's when I was caught off guard, this time I knew what was on the end of my line. I *wanted* it to be on the end of the line. I was ready for him. When I got him to the surface, I held the pole in the air with my left hand and picked up Daddy's pistol with my right. The snake was swinging back and forth at the end of the line, side to side like a pendulum. Then he started going around in a circle, and he was so mad he twisted his tail around and around himself until he almost tied himself in a knot, which was good because it made a better target. Calamity Jane couldn't have pulled off a better shot than I did. And it wasn't easy. I hit that swinging, writhing snake with one shot and he stopped moving, but I wasn't about to bring him back to the bank to check his pulse. I just cut the line and let him sink to the bottom and kept on fishing.

Mostly when I was little, we caught *little* fish, little bream, little perch, little mud cats. We weren't *trying* to catch *little* fish; we just fished for them in little places – little creeks and little ponds. After we moved to the fire station, Daddy got more sophisticated with his fishing. Up until then, we had always fished from the bank with cane poles. After Daddy got around the old fishing men at the fire station, I think he felt a little embarrassed that he was still sitting on the bank fishing with a cane pole, so he went out and bought himself a rod and reel and some artificial lures, little brightly painted wooden fish with hooks screwed into them, little fish that had intimidating names – Devil's Horse, Hula Popper, Bushwhacker, Nippa Diddy.

Daddy explained the concept to me. He said you stand on the bank or sit in a boat and sling the little wooden fish out as far as you could throw it and use the crank to pull it back in. And then you sling it again. And pull. Sling. Pull. That was it. You just keep slinging and cranking and sooner or later really big bass swim up and try to eat the wooden fish.

Well, I couldn't believe what I was hearing. It was clear to me that that piece of wood shaped like a fish wasn't real, and I was sure it would never fool a wary old bass. But Daddy swore it would and told me that that was how really big bass got caught. Not with cane poles and worms and minnows. I remained skeptical.

The first time Daddy used his new equipment, he didn't take me with him. I think he was a little skeptical about it too and was unsure of his slinging skills and didn't want to make a fool of himself in front of me.

One Sunday afternoon he drove over to a bar pit lake near the Pearl River. Like the Mississippi, when the Pearl over-flowed which it did just about every year, it filled the bar pit lakes with big fish, and left them there when the flood waters receded.

I sulked a little bit when Daddy left because he almost never went fishing without me.

He wasn't gone more than a few hours when he drove back in, honking the horn. I could tell from the look on his face that he was bustin' out proud. Daddy was hard to read non-verbally. His usual face was an impassive face, but that day when he got out of the car, he just couldn't keep from smiling – beaming actually.

He opened the trunk of the car and pulled out a stringer that had five big bass on it. Any one of them was bigger than any other fish either of us had ever caught. The biggest was five or six pounds and altogether he was holding probably fifteen pounds of bass. I was dumbstruck, not only by the number and size of the fish Daddy brought home, but by the realization that you really could fool a fish with a little piece of painted wood.

The next weekend he took me with him to a place where I could catch a bass too, but not using a rod and reel. I wasn't ready for that he said. We borrowed Red Myers's boat and headed toward Monticello to a small, nameless horseshoe-shaped lake called Snag Lake. For obvious reasons. It was a fisherman's dream lake and at the same time his or her worst nightmare lake. The surface was covered with cover – filled with stumps and logs and lily pads and water plants, every kind of place where fish loved to hide and every kind of place where fishermen were sure to hang their hooks. Beneath the surface it was even worse, a maze of unseen structure. It was a place where it would be easy to hook a fish and hell to get it in the boat.

It was soooo frustrating. I was at the front of the boat and Daddy was at the back, not so much paddling as pushing us from snag to snag to find a clear spot or to get our hooks un-hung. Just finding a spot to drop a hook in wasn't easy and I got hung up a half dozen times before I caught anything. It was useless for Daddy to even try to sling his wooden fish. When we could get a minnow down, we managed to catch a few slab crappie.

I can still close my eyes and see the place that I hung the big one that got away that day. Fallen tree trunks were crisscrossing and overlapping each other on the surface, forming a rectangle of open water. One of the logs had some kind of green water plant growing on it. I maneuvered my little minnow into the water beside that log and the very second it hit the water, it disappeared. I managed to override the impulse to jerk back the line and instead began pulling back with a steady even force. My bamboo pole bent almost double and my line started "singing," making a humming noise as it sliced the water. I managed to keep that fish in the box of open water and get him to the surface so we could see him. He was a magnificent bass. He was bigger than any Daddy had brought home and weighed. We guessed he'd go maybe eight or nine pounds. My heart was thump-lumping.

One of the advantages of hanging a big fish on a rod and reel as opposed to a cane pole is that you have a lot more line, can adjust the drag, and have more control. With a cane pole when a fish gets to the end of the line, that is pretty much it. When this fish was pulled out of his element into the air, he made another plunge for the bottom. I held on and tried to play him. We were having a tug of war and for a while I was winning. I got him back to the surface again, but instead of leaving him in the water and pulling him toward the boat, I lifted him up out of the water again. I was so stunned that I got him out without him wrapping the line around an under water obstacle that I paused too long with him dangling at the end of the line. For a split second he seemed equally stunned at being jerked into a world of sun and air, but he recovered and made his next move before I did. He curled his tail up toward his head and flipped it back again. With the combination of his weight and the sudden jerking motion he straightened my crappie hook and flopped back into the box of open water.

The words "Goddamn it, Daddy, he got away!!!" came out of my mouth as reflexively as a sneeze. And then I froze. I'd never even thought a cuss word before and now I had just taken the Lord's name in vain, which Mama said was the unforgivable sin that could consign you to the eternal fires and brimstone of hell if in fact God didn't strike you dead on the spot. I knew that was bad, but worse by far I had committed this sin in front of my Daddy. That could mean a punishment that was way worse than the fires of hell. My Daddy could tuck his chin down, pierce my soul with a look in his blue blue eyes that he got when he was really, really mad and say – nothing. Though my Daddy and his brothers and the men he knew and drank with cussed like professional cussers, good little Southern Baptist girls weren't supposed to utter even a plain "damn" much less the unforgivable sin version I'd just blurted out. And I was not only a good little Southern girl in the cultural sense, a good little Southern Baptist girl in the religious sense, I was the "good little girl" child of alcoholic parents – which meant that I tried to be perfect for them. Irrational as it was, I thought that if I were perfect they would love me enough not to drink and hurt me.

I expected an explosion of some kind from the back of the boat as I turned to face him. "I'm sorry, Daddy," I started to say, but when I looked at Daddy he was laughing. Really laughing. So I breathed again.

That was the first time and the last time I ever cussed in front of my Daddy. I was in my late thirties when Mama died and she never heard me cuss. Though for sure many others have.

I have recurring dreams. Not about bridges or snakes – but about fishing. In one I'm paddling a small boat slowly down Cocodrie Bayou, moving past cypress knees and lily pads and slider turtles, stopping here and there in fishy looking places, dropping my line in the dark water. In my dream I sit very still and stare at the cork, waiting and waiting, anticipating the movement. And in my dream I always get a bite, and the cork always goes under and I start to pull back and when I do I always wake up, never knowing what was on the end of my line. So the dream is always one of perpetual anticipation.

I first loved fishing because it was what Mama and Daddy and I did for fun when they were sober. Over time, long after their deaths, I realized that there is an even more basic reason why I love to fish. I am fundamentally a very optimistic person. Hope and anticipation have been the most positive driving forces in my life and fishing (and gambling for that matter) is an act of pure distilled hope and anticipation. I go to the water hoping I will catch the big one and I cast and reel or stare at my cork anticipating the tug or the big strike.

Or to put it another way. I love to fish because variable ratio payoffs are highly addictive.

I've tried and tried and for the life of me, I can't remember the *last* time I fished with my Daddy or the *last* time I went fishing with Mama. But it is just as well I can't. "Last time" memories are inherently sad and somehow fruitless, and I don't want to have a single, sad lingering memory of Mama and Daddy associated with fishing.

I just know that I'll never forget the *first* time I went fishing or that first little red-bellied sun perch and all the times in between the first and the last time I went fishing with Mama and Daddy, because they were the *best* times of my childhood, and to this day, the only thing that makes me *want* to get up and out of bed before sunrise is going fishing.

Working Girl

My Daddy was an alcoholic. He cursed like a sailor, had a quick-trigger temper, and he never went to church, except for funerals, and then only for blood relatives, not close friends. But by any other measure my Daddy was a *good* man. A truly honest and decent man. He wouldn't take a penny that wasn't his. He'd stop and help people in trouble along the road – help change their tire or get some gas for them and bring it back. He'd pick up hitchhikers, especially during the war when servicemen stood at crossroads thumbing their way home on furloughs. He forgave as many debts as he collected when he knew the debtor's needs were greater than his, and he did so without regard to the color of the man's skin. He was tough and stubborn, traits that he consciously tried to drill into me. One of the *games* he played with me, taken out of context, could in the mind of a suspicious social worker be regarded as some bizarre form of abuse, but he didn't mean it that way. He'd get some cans of fruit or vegetables – big cans. Then he'd tell me to stretch out my arms, palms up. Then he'd put the cans on my palms and he'd get out his pocket watch to see how long I could hold my arms up. It didn't take much weight or very long to reach the "I give up" place. When I'd held out my arms as long as I thought I could, I'd say,

"Daddy, I can't do it any more."

And he'd say, "hold 'em longer."

And I'd try harder and reach the giving up point again and again he'd say,

"Hold 'em longer."

As a game, the point of it all was to beat my own endurance time. As a lesson, it was to teach me to push myself beyond the easy stopping place. To this day I find Daddy's toughness and endurance training serves me well.

The Irish Crawfords on Mama's side of the family were all big talkers, big dreamers, gregarious, easy to laugh or cry or shout or hug and kiss you. They never met strangers. I know I got a lot of that from Mama, but my core is solid Meese and most of what I learned from Daddy; I learned from what he *did*, not what he *said*.

And what Gordon Meese did above all else was work hard. For all his drinking, he never, not once, missed a day of work because of it. In fact, the only time I can remember him not going to work for any reason was when he broke his leg dancing. That's right – dancing. He and Mama and some friends went down South of McComb and just across the state line into Louisiana to Uncle Bud's Honky Tonk for a night of drinking and dancing. The "Talk of the Town" gossip column in the *Brookhaven Leader Times* the next week carried a little blurb about Daddy's accident. The writer who was prone to use over-cooked prose noted that Gordon Meese broke his leg while "tripping the light fantastic."

Crawford men, other than Uncle Bud, were not known for being hard workers, so I guess I inherited a touch of the Quaker/ Puritan work ethic from the Meese side of my family and went to work too. When I was eight. Not because I had to, but because I wanted to. It made me feel independent.

My first job was collecting bills for Daddy. Roughly half of

Daddy's customers had charge accounts and Daddy, in turn, had an account with the Pure Oil distributor. He almost always had a cash flow problem because he *had* to pay Pure Oil on time or they wouldn't sell him any more gas. His customers weren't always so prompt.

Mama was the family bookkeeper. She had a little flip charge account book where she'd write down the customer's name and the amount of the charge. At night after they closed, Mama would tear off the day's charges and file them alphabetically and at the end of the month she'd add them all up and that was when the customer was supposed to pay the bill. About half of the charge customers did pay – faithfully – regularly – on time. Another few would come by and pay if Mama reminded them. Some would come by and explain why they couldn't pay right then and ask for a little more time. Others just stopped coming by altogether after running up a big bill, so Daddy was stiffed more times than I could count.

I don't see how he ever made any profit because he lost so much to bad debts, yet I never knew him to refuse to give credit to anyone. I don't think it was that he really trusted everyone so much as he was just one of those men who were unable to say "no." I also never heard him personally tell anyone he needed the money or ask them to pay their bill. Some men are just like that. Otherwise macho men who just wimped out when it came to dealing with other people.

Daddy never hired a lawyer, never sued anybody for not paying him, and never hired a collection agency to go after the bad debts. Instead, he hired me. When I was eight years old. From time to time, Mama pulled out a stack of what they considered uncollectibles and some from a few paying regulars and let me try to collect them. We had an unusual salary arrangement, but one that seemed appropriate between father and daughter. We agreed that every time I collected something, Daddy would get the dollars and I would get the cents. If the amount was $1.99, he got the dollar and I got ninety-nine cents; if it was $100.01, he got $100.00 and I got a penny.

I had two ways of going about my job. I'd either ride my bike over to the customer's house if they lived in town or walk around all the three main blocks of the downtown area on Saturday looking for the ones who came to town once a week to do their shopping. Using an eight-year-old to collect bills proved to be a pretty canny strategy. People who hid behind their curtains and doors and were always "gone" when grown-up bill collectors came around, would peep out, see a kid standing there and open the door. And when I walked around town and spotted a deadbeat on Saturday afternoon, even if he saw me coming, he couldn't very well take off running. How would that look? But they didn't want to stand around and argue with me either, because they wanted their encounter with the kid bill collector to be as quick and inconspicuous as possible. Besides they knew that everybody else knew when they saw me holding out my hand for some money what was going on, and that usually embarrassed even the deadest of the deadbeats.

Even as a child I didn't typically act on impulse, but pretty carefully thought through situations and made a plan before deciding on a course of action. Some who know this tendency of mine have called it *calculating*. I've always preferred a more benign characterization. To me it's a mix of problem-solving and planning, growing out of the notion that considering the consequences of an action *before* executing it is a prudent and wise thing to do.

Before I set out on my first collection round, I knew I couldn't just go up and say "give me my Daddy's money," so I considered my options. Clearly, force and intimidation as exemplified in gangster movies where the "enforcer" went out and broke the legs of weasels who didn't pay up on time were not choices open to me.

I couldn't imagine myself out right begging, even for what was rightfully Daddy's and by extension, mine.

I never went to anybody's house that didn't already know who I was, so I didn't have to introduce myself. I decided I'd just knock on the door, step back, put my hands behind my back and wait for someone to open the door. Then I'd bring out the charge tickets from behind my back, show them to him or her, look 'em right in the eye and say, "Mornin', ma'am or sir, I'm here because my Daddy needs the money you owe him." I'd pause, and then add, "I thought maybe you forgot about it, so I've come to get it."

If they claimed they couldn't pay it all, which was often the case, I'd try to negotiate a partial payment. I'd thank them, put the money in my pocket and head back to the station. They usually looked puzzled when, because of the pay arrangement I had with Daddy, I asked them to add some cents to any amount they offered to pay. If they wanted to give me $5.00, I'd push for $5.50, and if they couldn't go up, I'd go down and counter with, "Well, how about $4.75 then?"

One of my favorite regular stops was with an elderly black woman who lived back behind the barbershop in the Quarters. Hattie didn't drive. In fact she didn't own a car, but she "stood good" for her son Deberry, who at one time had worked for Daddy for a little while. Deberry was a charming, roguish, womanizing man who held no job for long and considered his debts as something to be forgiven by Biblical injunction – just like it said in the Lord's prayer.

From time to time when he had been kicked out of his latest girlfriend's house and wasn't in jail, Deberry would come live with Hattie and sponge off her for awhile. Then he'd find another woman to take him in, "borrow" some money from his Mama's little hidden stash and take off again with promises to get a job, go to church, and thank the Lord for his blessings.

Hattie paid Daddy a little something every month for Deberry, and I went to get it. Some of my "clients" knew when they opened the door that I was there to dun them and didn't always greet me with a smile. But Hattie did. Most of the time she lived alone and was lonely, so she was glad to have anybody come knocking on her door and welcomed me more as if I were just stopping by to visit than coming as a bill collector.

Hattie walked four blocks every morning to the corner of old South Highway 51 where a local doctor's wife picked her up and took her to her home to wash her dishes, iron her clothes, push her baby around the block in a buggy, and cook enough supper to take some home for herself, feed the doctor's wife and baby and leave enough on the stove for the doctor when he managed to get home from his hospital rounds and house calls.

Hattie had to walk to the corner to meet the doctor's wife, rain or shine, July and December because her white employer wouldn't drive down into the Quarters. I think Hattie liked my visits because I rode my bicycle to her house and went in "to set a spell" when she invited me to, though anything that smacked of socializing between whites and blacks was taboo back then. Between adults. Even then children didn't always live within absolute racial boundaries.

It just seemed the most natural and polite thing to do. I did it all the time at Ella May's when I worked my other job – my sales job. Back then, when folks had some old clothes or discarded household goods they wanted to sell, they had a *rummage* sale, not a *garage* sale or a *yard* sale, but a *rummage* sale. Nobody had rummage sales in their own yards, in front of their own homes. It would have just been too tacky to put your used stuff out in front of your own house and haggle with people over its residual value. Even if you did, nobody in your own neighborhood would dare to be seen in a neighbor's yard buying their old stuff. And the neighbors would have been outraged if anyone had put up signs and invited the people who might actually want and need to buy your stuff to come into their neighborhood. So rummage sales were typically held on Saturday afternoons when country folks and all the black folks from the Quarters came to town. They were held downtown on empty street corners, vacant lots or the grassy area in the Railroad Park across from City Hall and the A & P.

I got so good at bill collecting that I decided to branch out into the rummage sale business. One of the best sale sites was a vacant corner lot diagonally across the street from Daddy's station, directly across from the First Baptist Church and Keys Motor Company. It was ideal because lots of people passed by there, Mama and Daddy could see me at all times, and they could direct customers to head across the street and check out my merchandise.

Mostly I sold used clothes; Mama's because she was something of a clothes-horse and didn't like to wear the same outfit for more than a season, mine because I outgrew my clothes so fast. Not by getting fatter, just taller and skinnier.

I never had any men's things to sell because Daddy wore all clothes until they were completely "wore out." Besides, he never really wore anything but khaki uniforms and a cap with a bill on it like the ones policemen wore. For my entire life to that point, Daddy only owned one white shirt at a time, one old brown suit, one pair of "sports" pants and a shirt to go with it. He had two pairs of shoes and a beat up old felt hat that he wore for funerals. Though he rarely ever wore them, he had a lot of neckties mainly because I kept giving them to him as presents for his birthday and Father's Day and Christmas because that's what you gave daddies back then.

Once, years later, after he was diagnosed with prostate cancer and mellowed a little bit, we chartered a day of deep-sea fishing down at Gulfport and Mama bought Daddy a pair of blue Bermuda shorts to wear. He was self-conscious all day long and he never wore them again. It was the only time in my life I ever saw my Daddy's bare legs. They were funny looking legs. Scrawny. And the whitest legs I had ever seen.

I usually talked Mama into discarding some of her old figurines or a few pieces of costume jewelry or a pot or pan just to add some variety to my sale merchandise. I held a couple of sales on the corner and did pretty well, netting three or four dollars each time. Then I made an important marketing decision. I decided to take my goods to where the customers lived instead of waiting for them to pass by me.

I began going to Ella May's house in the quarters to have my sales. Mama would help me pack up everything in cardboard boxes and take it over to Ella May's early Saturday morning and come back and get me mid-afternoon. I hung some of my clothes on the limbs of her chinaberry tree and draped some over the chicken wire fence around the yard. Then Ella May and I'd sit on her front porch steps and drink Kool-Aid and eat Red Hots cinnamon candy and wait for customers to start stirring. There was always a bunch of lookers who came early and pretended to be thinking about buying something. Most of them never intended to buy anything. They just came because it was something to do and to see for themselves if it was true that a little white child was spending the day in the quarters.

To stir up interest and drum up some action and business, I'd walk around every half hour or so in every direction away from Ella May's house like a seasoned street vendor, yelling "ruuuuuuuummmmmmmmage sale…rummmmmaaaaggge sale" with a rhythmic intonation that I used trying to imitate the sound of the men who came through town from time to time pushing a cart with a whetstone wheel they used to sharpen knives and scissors.

Business was usually best right after I first set up. We had a fairly steady stream of Ella May's neighbors until lunchtime. Then things slowed down. Instead of the three or four dollars I'd been making downtown, at Ella May's I sold as much as ten dollars worth of stuff at a time, which was a fortune to a child back then.

One of my best customers had a little girl just a little younger and smaller than I was and she bought all my best clothes. She'd always sit down and talk to Ella May and me for awhile, and we'd offer her some Kool-Aid and Red Hots. One time when she came, she was a lot bigger than I'd ever seen her before and she walked slower and sat down more heavily.

For some reason *pregnant* was a word that adults did not use in front of children back then, so when I said something to Ella May about how fat her friend was getting, she just turned away and didn't answer me. But not long after that Ella May told me her friend had a new baby. Another little girl child.

"And guess what she named that baby?" she asked me.

I just shrugged my shoulders.

"She named that baby Jimmie Francis," she told me. "She named that baby for you, honey. Ain't that special?"

I was genuinely proud to know there was a baby in the world that was named after me. I sensed that it was somehow a great compliment. Most of my friends had names that other people had too. I knew lots of *Anns, Marys, Susans*, and *Fayes*. I even knew two people named *Maxine*. But I thought I was the only living girl on earth named Jimmie. Though I didn't like my name at all, I always got angry and defensive when people teased me about it. And when someone said something really stupid about my name, like "your parents wanted a boy, huh?" I always shot back, "No! I was named for my dead aunt, Jimmie Lonnie Tickle Crawford. I don't *know* what her Mama and Daddy wanted."

Some people begin searching for names nine months before their baby is born. Others, like my Daddy, pick their baby's name years ahead of time and regardless of the sex of the child, use it. My Daddy picked my name all by himself eighteen years before I was born. Here's how he did it.

My Daddy was seven years older than my Mama and when he was nineteen and she was twelve he ran around with her older brothers, Lonnie Frank, Floyd Bud, Grady, Ed, and Hebo.

The way I heard it, one of the girls that ran around with Daddy and all my uncles was named Jimmie Lonnie – Jimmie Lonnie Tickle. She wasn't even Daddy's girlfriend; she was Uncle Grady's. In fact, Uncle Grady married her. It seems Daddy just thought that Jimmie Lonnie Tickle was the cutest, sweetest girl he'd ever met, and I guess he must have really loved her name because he decided when my Mama was only twelve years old that when he got married, if he did, and when they had a baby, if they did – that baby would be named Jimmie Lonnie. Boy or girl, his first baby would be named Jimmie Lonnie. Period. End of discussion.

Six years later, when Mama was eighteen, she gave up her dream of going to Secretary School and ran off and married Gordon Eli Meese. Twelve years later – eighteen years after Daddy named me – I was finally born.

I often wondered if Mama liked my name or had a problem with her only daughter being named after a pretty girl her husband had once admired. I wondered too what she would have named me if she had had any say so in the matter.

I never knew the lady I was named for. Jimmie Lonnie Tickle Crawford died three months after marrying Uncle Grady. She's buried in the Crawford plot at Sylvarena Baptist Church. Sometimes Mama and I went to Sylvarena for revivals and family reunions. Once when we went to church there, Mama walked me out through the cemetery to show me where Big Daddy and Big Mama were buried. I'd forgotten that the lady I was named for was buried there too and was spooked when I stumbled over a tombstone with my name on it.

For the longest time, I never knew another female Jimmie and was pretty sure that the dead Jimmie Lonnie Tickle Crawford, the little black Jimmie Francis, and I, Jimmie Lonnie Meese, were the only girl Jimmies on earth.

I loved doing my rummage sale and bill collecting jobs. I used my money to go to two double feature matinee cowboy movies every Saturday afternoon, buy Red Hots at Panzica's grocery every day, and a milkshake from the ice cream factory around the block from the station a couple of times week.

My friends were always impressed that I earned my own money and didn't have to ask Mama and Daddy every time I wanted something, though as far as I know, none of them were ever impressed enough to get a job of their own. Or maybe, for some reason their parents wouldn't let them. My Mama and Daddy were proud of my work ethic, and I loved it when they bragged about what a hard little worker I was.

When I was ten or eleven, I got my first *real job*, a job working in a real shop on a regular schedule for a regular salary. Mr. Lankford, who owned Lankford's Shoe Shop, had always doted on me. He was a well-educated man, more like a professor than a cobbler, and I swear he looked just like Geppetto in Pinocchio. He had a round sweetly benign face, rimless glasses that were always perched on the tip of his nose so he could lower his head and look over them, and he almost always had on a long brown heavy canvas apron. His shop was just two stores down from Daddy's service station with only Paul Sartain's Fish Market between them.

One day, Mr. Lankford, out of the blue, saw me and asked me to come down to his shop when I could because he had something he wanted to talk to me about. I hated even walking past Paul's Fish Market. It stunk. I tried to hold my breath when I got within fifteen feet of the place. I felt bad too because Paul of Paul's Market only hauled the fish in once a week while his wife, Pauline, was the one who was always trapped in there, scaling and gutting cold fish all day long. She was a real nice lady, always smiling and friendly, and calling out to me when she saw me go by, and I felt bad because I always tried to avoid her because she smelled so much like week-old fish, which even when kept on ice got pretty rank.

As much as I hated the fish market, I loved going to Mr. Lankford's shop because it always smelled of new leather and paste shoe polish. I told Mama Mr. Lankford asked me to come talk to him and we were both curious about what he wanted. When I got to his shop, he motioned for me to sit down. Just to the left of the front door there were two little box-like enclosures with hinged gates. When customers came in and wanted to *wait* to get their shoes fixed instead of leaving them, they sat barefooted in the little boxes. That day Mr. Lankford sat down in one of the little boxes and motioned for me to sit in the other one.

Over in the work area, Porter and Johnny were thumping around, leaning on a crutch with one hand and working with the other, holding shoes against one of the wheels on the long bank of rotating brushes and sanders and stitching and cutting machines. Porter and Johnny were both one-legged black men. Porter had lost his right leg at the knee and Johnny had lost his left one (or maybe it was the other way around) at about the same place and they wore the same size shoe, so they wore one pair of shoes between them, and they had lots and lots of fancy shoes. When customers left their shoes for too long – like more than three months, Mr. Lankford took them off the pick-up rack and gave them to Porter and Johnny. They didn't care how big they were, just so they weren't too small. They would wear anything on their good foot, from a size seven to a size twelve.

Mr. Lankford was a big talker and he used bigger words and sounded a whole lot smarter than most of the people who ran shops in Brookhaven. I suspected that he'd been to college, though I wasn't sure exactly what college was all about since neither Mama nor Daddy had ever been to one. I just knew it was something that smart people went to and decided I would go to one too.

Mr. Lankford led off with, "I've been watching you for a long time, young lady."

That wasn't what I had expected him to say and I wasn't sure how to respond, so I paused for a second or two, kept looking him in the eye and asked what seemed to me the most logical question.

"Why?"

Mr. Lankford never answered a question directly or approached a subject head on like Daddy did. He talked around and about for a long time before he got to where he was going.

"Well, you know Miz Lankford has been ill a lot this year."

I noticed that he said *ill* instead of *sick*, which is what everybody else I knew would have said. That was what I meant about him using bigger words than most people. I didn't mean that the words were necessarily longer or had more letters and syllables in them, because *ill* only has three letters and *sick* has four, but *ill* sounded like a big word when Mr. Lankford said it. I mentioned this to Mama that night and she agreed that Mr. Lankford had probably gone to college, but she reckoned that he probably talked like he did because she thought he had been born in some place like Vermont or New Hampshire and was thus a Yankee. I pointed out that he drawled out words just like everybody else, but she said it didn't matter if he *talked* Southern, what made you a Yankee was where you were born. Like Daddy being born in Danville, Illinois. I had to think about that for a long time. Somehow it didn't seem fair. It seemed to me like you ought to be able to outgrow what you were born as.

"Yes, sir, how's she doin'?"

"It's hard to say. I believe that the real problem is that she's just tired coming down here everyday. She wants to make a quilt. And she wants to go to her sister's house and Christmas is only three weeks away and we've not yet mailed our Christmas cards." (Most folks would have said "mailed our Christmas cards *yet*" not "*yet* mailed our Christmas cards.")

The more Mr. Lankford talked, the more confused I got. It seemed really important to him that I know Miz Lankford wanted to make a quilt and he was obviously distressed about his Christmas cards, but I had no idea what any of this had to do with *me*.

So I just kept on looking him in the eye and nodding my head.

Then, all of a sudden he changed rhetorical directions and got to the point of it all. "Would you like to come and work for me and earn some money for Christmas?"

That became the pattern for all conversation with Mr. Lankford – the way he thought and the way he talked. He'd head off on what seemed to be a totally unrelated subject and then abruptly stop, reverse course and utter one simple clear summative sentence that actually made sense and tied all the other broken threads together. (Much much later I learned that he was actually creating something called a *chain of logical necessity.*)

It was the phrase "earn some money" that caught my attention. While I still didn't understand what he expected me to do, I was already ready to say "yes" but I knew that I'd have to talk to Mama and Daddy before I could answer him and started to tell him that, when he added,

"Now I know that you are going to have to discuss this with your Mother and Father, so you tell them I want you to work as my cashier and address my Christmas cards and that I'll pay you well."

"Okay, sure, Mr. Lankford," I jumped up and started for the door. "Thank you, sir. I"ll be back."

"Mama, Mama!" I hit the service station in high gear. "Mr. Lankford wants me to work for him for money. Can I? Can I? Can I?"

Of course she asked more questions than I had answers for. When would I work? What would I do? She tried to point out what she saw as drawbacks to the proposition. Not because she opposed it, but because she wanted me to really think about all that it would entail. She told me I would have to wait until she talked to Mr. Lankford to get more details and that I couldn't do it unless Daddy agreed.

Mama was satisfied with Mr. Lankford's answers. Daddy not only agreed, he was proud of me. Of course, he didn't tell me he was proud of me, I just overheard him tell Slim, a big tall guy that worked at the station for a few years. They were out under the grease rack changing oil in a pulp wood truck when out of the blue, Daddy said something. I think that's what caught my attention. He barely answered when Mama talked to him, and he almost never was the first to speak to anyone, and here he was, in his way, bragging about me to Slim.

"Jim's gonna work at the Shoe Shop,"

"Sho nuff, Mr. Gordon. Ain't she somethin'?

"Yeah, she is."

It turned out to be a pretty easy job. I worked for Mr. Lankford all day on Saturday, putting my movie matinees on hiatus and after school on Wednesday. I earned $5.00 a week.

For that magnificent sum, I sat on a tall stool behind the counter and the cash register, greeted customers, took in the shoes that were left for repairs, and marked the claim check to show what the customer wanted done. Full soles? Half soles? Heels? Neolite? Rubber? Leather? Shine? Taps? I'd recite the litany of options and services.

When customers came in for pickups, I took their claim ticket and checked the racks with finished jobs for a matching number. I'd always ask customers if they needed any shoestrings or polish, then I'd tell them how much they owed, take their money, give them their change, thank them for coming and ask them to come back soon. Unlike Daddy, Mr. L, as I started calling him, was a good businessman. He didn't allow anybody to pay on credit. If someone who looked to be down on his or her luck came in with worn down shoes, he might do it for free, but he didn't charge anything to anybody. I told Daddy he should make everybody pay cash too.

Mr. L was always there on Saturday to work along side Porter and Johnny, but he never stood over me and checked on what I was doing. He trusted everything he had to me. On Wednesday afternoons when we weren't busy like we were on Saturdays he would often take off to go to the bank or run some errands. When he left, he left me in charge.

As long as there were customers coming in and out and I stayed busy, I liked what I was doing, but when there was nothing to do but sit on the stool and wait, I'd get restless and bored and count the hours, and in the last hour of the day, the minutes until it was quitting time.

The first Wednesday afternoon I worked, Mr. L got out all his Christmas cards and gave me a long list of names and addresses and asked me to write them on the envelopes as prettily and neatly as I could. I didn't have to sign them for him because he had them printed and inside in red ink he'd written: *Lankford's Shoe Shop appreciates your business and wishes you a Merry Christmas!* Most of the people on his list were customers and had Brookhaven addresses, but some were to other people named Lankford in places like New Hampshire and Connecticut where he said they had white Christmases every year.

Looking at all those pictures of snow covered trees and churches and sleighs and ice skaters on the cards got me in the mood for Christmas. When I went to do my Christmas shopping that year, I bought Daddy a box of white handkerchiefs with an "M" on them and a key ring. Every year when you asked Daddy what he wanted, all he ever said was handkerchiefs, but I always wanted to get him a surprise too. Mama always got him undershirts and shorts.

That year when I went to the men's department at McGrath's Ready to Wear Shop to get Daddy's gift, I took a little time and looked around at all the other things they had for men. I was looking at the wallets and belts and things made of leather to put on desks when I saw a man, someone I didn't even know, standing in front of a mirror on a stool while another man knelt down and put pins in the bottom of his pant's legs. I'd never seen a grown man do anything like that before and thought it was very odd. Then the kneeling man got up and helped him put on a coat that matched the pants. I'd also never seen a man preening in front of a mirror like the man on the stool did. I could tell that he really liked the way he looked because of the way he ran his hand through his hair and tilted his head from side to side as he studied the effect.

He looked just like one of the models I'd seen in the Sears-Roebuck catalog. I decided right then that I was gonna buy my Daddy a suit like that. I waited around until the man went into the dressing room and the sales guy was by himself.

I guess he could tell by the way I approached him that I needed help.

"Merry Christmas, little lady, can I help you?"

"Yes sir. I was looking for something to buy my Daddy for Christmas."

"And do you have something special in mind?"

"Well, I'd like to get him one of those suits like that man had on."

Deep down I was pretty sure that I didn't have enough money to buy it, but I figured if he thought I wanted to, he'd have to at least tell me how much it cost."

"Good choice, little lady. That is our top of the line."

"My name is Jimmie," I said.

"Excuse me," he said.

"You keep calling me little lady. My name is Jimmie. Can you tell me how much that top of your line suit costs?'

"That one is $120.00."

I almost fell over. I had no idea men paid that much money for something to wear, and I knew right then that I could never buy Daddy a top-of-the-line suit, but I didn't give up that fast.

"Well, sir, how much is one of your bottom-of-the-line suits?"

His real customer started coming out of the dressing room and the clerk was now certain that spending more time with me was a waste, but he was a polite man.

"Over there," he said and pointed to another rack. "$55.00. Take a look at them."

That's when I started to hatch another plan. I knew there was no way I could come up with $50.00 that close to Christmas, but now that I had a real job I could count on, I decided to just go ahead with the handkerchief and key ring and to come back after the holidays and get Daddy something really special for the next Christmas.

I also knew I would need Mama's help for this plan, so early in January I told her what I wanted to do and asked her to go with me back to McGrath's to get something really nice for Daddy for the next Christmas. She might have had some reservation about the ambitiousness of my project or whether I could stick with the plan for a whole year, but at her best Mama was a super enabler.

The same salesman greeted Mama and me. I think he remembered me, but he focused all his attention and addressed all his questions to Mama. To make sure he knew I was the customer he needed to be talking to, not Mama, I said,

"Sir, I want to put one of your bottom-of-the-line suits on lay-away for my Daddy."

When I said that, he looked at Mama and she nodded to affirm that I was indeed the customer. He shifted gears fast and starting paying attention to me. I always got a kick out of that kind of response – watching people first underestimate you and then start sucking up when they found out you had good sense or some money or you had something they wanted.

It turned out that the bottom-of-the-line suits were now on sale for $42.50, so Mama helped with the size and I picked out a gray, double-breasted suit. With the savings on the suit, I decided that Daddy needed a new felt hat too, so I got him a felt hat, just like the one he always wore only darker gray, with a black band that had a little blue feather in it. Then figuring that I'd have a whole year to come up with the money, I went "whole hog" and picked him out a white shirt and a new tie.

The man explained to Mama that because of store policy he couldn't put a $60.00 order on lay away for a ten-year-old child. He'd have to put it under her name. Mama said that was all right, but he should understand that I would be the one coming by to make the regular payments on it. He said that would be fine. So for the next year I checked in shoes and sold shoe polish and shoelaces and took money to the man at McGraths's.

As the next Christmas season rolled around and the amount due on my layaways was down to a few dollars, I had an awful thought. A terrible, horrible, awful thought. I was ready to give my Daddy a whole new outfit so he could look proud like the man in the mirror, and all I would have for Mama would be the same old Coty's Gift Pack or a string of some kind of cheap beads.

So I hatched another plan. I went on a browsing tour of the jewelry stores in town. I just went in and walked round and round the counters, checking out the ladies watches and pointing now and then to one and asking the price. Most of the clerks, like the man at McGrath's, didn't waste any of their sales patter on me, but they would tell me a price when I asked. When I got to Brown's Jewelry, it was different. The owner was the only person working there and he was really more a watch repairman than a jewelry salesman. He was a bald-headed man with thick glasses and a little telescope sticking out from the top of his head and he reminded me of a unicorn.

I walked around looking in all the display cases and pointing at watches and asking prices. I thought everything was either too tacky or cost too much until I noticed a little yellow gold watch with a simple band at the back of the case. Mr. Brown said it was only $39.00. Even though I'd worked a whole year to pay for my Daddy a suit of clothes, I knew that no grown-up in his right mind would open up an outright charge account for a child.

I stared at the watch some more, thanked Mr. Brown and left. I started to go buy Mama some perfume a time or two, but couldn't stop thinking about the gold watch, so I just kept putting off buying her anything. A few days before Christmas, Aunt Bess, Mama's sister, came from Houston to spend Christmas with family. Like all of Mama's sisters and brothers, except Aunt Edna and Uncle Grady, she had no children of her own. Aunt Bess looked kind of like I think Mama would have looked if you cut her off at the knees. Mama was 5'10 and Aunt Bess was barely 5'2". They were both fussy about the way they looked and both smoked a lot and drank a lot and laughed a lot. It would be easy to paint Aunt Bess as some kind of flamboyant Auntie Mame, but that would be overstating it. She was, however, bawdy and fun and took me over as if I belonged to her when she was in town, and I loved it.

As soon as Aunt Bess and I were alone, I hatched another plan. I told her about what I had bought Daddy for Christmas and what I wanted to buy Mama and asked her to go with me to the jewelry store to look at the watch and "stand good" for me like Hattie did for Deberry so I could buy Mama a gold watch on credit.

She agreed. When we got there, Mr. Brown looked up, recognized me and smiled. I said, "Mr. Brown, this is my Aunt Bess Davis from Houston, Texas, and she's got something to tell you." Aunt Bess, who was always bragging about me, told Mr. Brown what a "responsible, hardworking, reliable" child I was and what I had done for Daddy. She told him I wanted to buy the watch, but didn't have enough money and asked if he would charge it to me, with the understanding that she would "stand good" for my debt if I failed to repay it fully. I'm not sure whether Mr. Brown was more impressed with my Puritan work ethic or by Aunt Bess' spiel and the way she had of flirting a little bit with every man she met, but he agreed to do it and I left the store with a gold watch for my Mama and a debt that would keep me working for Mr. L well into the next year.

I always loved wrapping Christmas presents. I bought some red ribbon and some paper with Santa Claus faces all over it and sat down on the floor to wrap presents while Aunt Bess sat at the table and drank coffee and smoked cigarettes and gave me encouragement and kept telling me how she wished she had a child of her own, just like me.

"Do you think they're gonna like their presents?" I asked her over and over.

It's funny how you remember some things and forget other important things that happened in your life. When I try to remember specific gifts that I *received* that Christmas, I draw a complete blank, but the memory of seeing my Mama and Daddy open their gifts that year is as clear and indelibly etched on my mind as my memory of what I had for breakfast this morning.

Mama, of course, raved and raved and called Cat and Irma to brag about her gift. Daddy opened his packages and looked at his suit and then looked at me for a long time. I smiled at him and said, "I bought it all by myself, Daddy!" He whispered a little thank you and got up and went in the bedroom, took out his handkerchief and wiped his eyes and blew his nose.

For a long time after that, the only suit Daddy ever wore was the one I gave him when I was eleven years old and Mama wore her watch until it stopped ticking.

They loved their gifts and wanted to show them off. Other than fishing with him, my favorite thing to do with Daddy was play Barber Shop, so that Christmas day Daddy got out his razor and lather brush and sat down and let me shave him and comb his hair. Then he put on all his new clothes and we drove up close to "It" to visit Aunt Blanche and Uncle Lish Massey.

Aunt Blanche was surprised to see us and couldn't believe that

Daddy was all dressed up in a suit and tie, and when I told her that I worked and bought it for him, she couldn't stop 'mirating (colloquial for *admiring*) over what I'd done. Aunt Blanche brought out her fruit cake for Mama and Daddy and some star-shaped sugar cookies for me and Uncle Lish, who had a big flappy wattle like a tom turkey's that hung from his chin to his Adam's apple, played the piano and we sang Christmas carols.

This is the only Christmas memory I can bring myself to write about. It is a sterling memory. Unlike just about every other Christmas in my childhood, Mama and Daddy were sober all day.

Stinky Won!

*I*n addition to my jobs as a professional bill collector, salesgirl, and cashier, I also earned a little money as a tout for a local politician.

When Uncle Frank built his rental property across the street from the fire station and City Hall, he built a duplex and two identical garage apartments. Not long after we moved into one of the garage apartments, Lyda and Ralph D. "Stinky" Martin moved next door and we became good friends and good neighbors in every sense of the word.

Lyda was a nurse. She was tall as a model and walked with the straight-backed shoulders of a proud person, like Mama was always, always after me to do. She had snappy black eyes and black hair with lots of body so it did just what she wanted it to do. When she put on her stiff-starched, bright white nurses uniform and cap, I thought she was just the prettiest person I'd ever seen standing right in front of me – almost as pretty as my favorite movie actress, Jennifer Jones.

Stinky was, as I recall, shorter than Lyda and I think a lot older. Whatever age he was, he looked old to me because his head was egg-shaped and bald on top and all bald headed men seemed really old to me. And he was what we then called cock-eyed. When one of his eyes was looking straight ahead, the other one was kind of looking off to the side.

He worked at Uncle Frank's funeral home as what some people called a "grief man." He and Dewey Jackson were considered two of the best in the professional consoler business. If you lived in Brookhaven and were important in any way, say a deacon in your church or a pharmacist or wrote a column for the local paper and you died, the family definitely wanted Stinky and Dewey to be the ones to ready you for viewing. They worked magic in the embalming room, managing to pull twisted smiles on to the lips of even the sourest old grumps. The finishing touches were usually applied by the oldest May sister, the one who now regularly fried my hair. She was called in for hair combing and curling, shaving and make-up. She was good at what she did too, though most people thought she went a little too heavy on the red lipstick – especially on the men. Rather than leaving her "special customers" with a life-like natural quality, she usually rolled them out looking like they'd just been sucking on a cherry popsicle.

After helping the families choose suitable *arrangements*, they rolled the body out into one of the grief salons and stood by respectfully greeting mourning friends, consoling family members, and placing wreaths artfully around the room with the élan of British butlers, all the while whispering like they were in the library or as if they were afraid they'd wake up the one who had gone on to meet his or her maker. They hugged every woman and patted her on the back and solemnly shook hands with every man. With Stinky the hugging and patting was sincere and natural; with Dewey it sometimes seemed like he really didn't enjoy hugging crying people for a living. He was basically cut from the same male cloth as Daddy, and he for sure didn't go home hugging and patting and being sensitive to his wife, Mama's friend Cat.

When there were no mourners in the funeral home, it was just like any other normal place of business. Stinky and Dewey took off their suit coats and sat around with the other guys and chewed gum and smoked cigarettes and told lies and played practical jokes on each other. But let a bona fide mourner anywhere near them and they snapped into grief gear without missing a beat.

In Brookhaven, in the '40s, you were sometimes more closely connected with your neighbors than you were with blood relatives – especially with cousins two and three times removed that you only saw at funerals and family reunions, the ones who always called you by your whole name just to prove they really knew you. The phrase "mi casa – su casa" was literally true for good neighbors. With only twenty steps or so between our stairs and Lyda and Stinky's, few days ever passed that we weren't in and out of each other's houses and lives in one way or another. Now that people literally live with little cell phone receivers stuck in their ear and walk around talking when clearly nobody is with them, it's hard to believe, but when we lived next door to Lyda and Stinky we didn't even have a telephone in our house. We used theirs. Whether they were at home or not. Same thing with eggs and milk or sugar, whatever one of us ran out of, we borrowed from the other. Whether they were at home or not.

Once when Harold Lofton, a Brookhaven football player, made high school All-American and played in an all-star game in Memphis, Lyda and Stinky took me with them to watch the game. We rode "The City of New Orleans" train up to Memphis and Mama made me a pretty linen skirt and bought me a yellow dotted Swiss blouse to wear with it. I got ready at least two hours early and stood at the door waiting for Lyda and Stinky to come out of their house to walk up to the train station. When I saw them come out, I got so excited, I kissed Mama goodbye as she started going through her "Do-Not List." I started running down the garage apartment steps.

Mama was standing in the living room saying, "Now you

hold Lyda's hand – do not let her out of your sight – do not – do not – do not...." I, of course, was only half listening, saying "yes ma'am, yes ma'am" and looking back at Mama when I hit the stairs going so fast that somehow the top part of my body couldn't keep up with the momentum of the bottom half. I lost my balance, fell backwards and bounced down two or three steps on my butt. Unfortunately, Uncle Frank's maintenance man had just replaced some of the boards on the steps using wood treated with black stinky creosote.

My new linen skirt was ruined and Mama was at the top of the steps screaming like she'd been the one who had fallen. Mama would have for sure pinched her lips and hummed sad hymns with a fury if she'd had me all alone, but Lyda and Stinky were standing at the bottom of the steps trying to comfort and reassure me, so Mama just called me back in and pulled out something else for me to wear. She didn't fuss at me then. In fact, she didn't say anything, but using all her considerable non-verbal skill, she made it clear that she was really mad at me and that I would hear hummed hymns for a long time after I got back home.

As always when I thought about trains leaving Brookhaven going North, I remembered the day Sister Clare left town, but even that thought and the sense of foreboding I usually had when I knew Mama's humming punishment was looming faded away as soon as Lyda and Stinky and I and a slew of other Harold Lofton fans got on the train heading for Memphis. Lyda and Stinky, who never had any children of their own, doted on me and made me feel like I was their daughter for a day. Mama had given me money to pay my own way, but Stinky paid for everything – including the fried chicken and ice cream we ate in the dining car on a table with a white tablecloth.

Every single person in Harold's fan club knew and loved Stinky Martin. When he was not being "somber man" at the funeral home, he was a great teller of jokes and tall tales. After lunch he and some important men sat around and smoked cigars and talked about football and politics. Lyda let me sit in the seat next to the window and I did nothing but look out the window as we rolled through hill country and then the Delta passing pastures and cows and cotton.

In his job at the funeral home, Stinky had hugged just about every neck, patted just about every back, and shaken just about every hand in Brookhaven – more than once. He knew everybody's first and middle name and always greeted them appropriately and respectfully, using the formal *Mr.* and *Miz* with all adults – even the buddies he hunted and fished with, and a subtlely subservient tone with the important people in Brookhaven and lots of Ma'ams and Sirs with everyone he suspected of being older than he was. He also knew everyone's children's and grandchildren's name, when they were graduating and where they were going to college, and on the darker side he knew which young girls were sent out of town for six or eight months and came back looking slimmer and subdued and sad.

In short, Stinky knew everybody and everybody who knew Stinky liked him. Not long after our trip to Memphis, it dawned on Stinky that he had what everyone who ever runs for public office wants more than anything else: name recognition, a high approval rating and a ready made, grass roots support system. Stinky decided to run for Tax Assessor. He didn't have to quit his job to run, so he kept on patting and hugging people at the funeral home. Since the funeral home was directly across the street from City Hall, Stinky could spot all the important people coming and going there, and when he didn't have "guests in the parlor," the funeral home guys' euphemism for dead people in the building, he'd go over and do a little politicking with them.

Before Stinky ran for Tax Assessor, everything I knew about politics was filtered through Mama and Daddy and their political perspective was an odd mixture of duty, distrust and secrecy. There were four absolutes in my parent's view of politics: (1) most politicians for any office were corrupt and *all* candidates for sheriff were, (2) never discuss politics with anyone, especially paying customers, (3) never ever tell anyone who you were going to vote for, and (4) after the election, always claim to have voted for whoever won.

Premise one was based on the notion that pretty much everyone wanted to be able to buy whiskey and drink it. They just didn't want to be able to buy it legally and drink it openly. To accomplish this milestone of hypocrisy, Mississippi institutionalized the sale of bootleg liquor with a smoke-and-mirror system whereby the state taxed and collected revenue from the sale of alcohol without legalizing the sale of it. This created a grand illusion that protected everyone. Mississippi remained nominally a dry state; the Baptists collectively and the teetotalers individually could hide their eyes and pretend that Mississippi was really a dry state; the state derived revenue from the bootleggers, and the drunks and hell-raisers could keep on driving to their local "legger," honk the horn and get drive-through service.

I'm sure there were Mayors and Councilmen who served the city well from a real sense of public service, but usually the man who was elected sheriff was the one who most successfully embodied the hypocrisy of the system. They typically voted for someone who could raise hell and get knee-walking drunk on Saturday night but sober up enough on Sunday morning to get to his church pew before nodding off to sleep again. The hypocrites' ideal candidate was a church-going man who the deacons could vote for, a drinking man who knew where all the bootleggers lived, and a bribe taking man who could expect more than a little campaign support from them in exchange for letting them stay in business. A win-win-win situation if ever there was one. All it took to perpetuate the system was everyone pretending it didn't exist or if they did admit it existed, quickly adding, "I, of course, am opposed to it."

I'm sure that Daddy, who knew where every bootlegger lived in Lincoln and Copiah County – white or black – favored the status quo. Every drink I ever saw him take was swigged straight from a bottle that was stuck inside a brown paper bag. Swigged furtively. Guiltily. Not because the booze was illegal in Mississippi, but because it was the tangible evidence of his weak will. I don't think Daddy knew what a social drink or a mixed drink was.

The second truism of Mama and Daddy's political philosophy was never discuss politics with anyone, especially anyone who buys gas from you, or anyone who someday might buy gas from you, or anyone who used to buy gas from you and still owes you money. The idea was to live your life without ever making anybody mad at you. In the same vein, they were so closed about who they were voting for that they wouldn't even tell each other.

All in all, there was very little conversation around our house about politics and what there was, was pretty negative.

That all changed when Stinky decided to run for Tax Assessor. Stinky was our next-door-neighbor. Stinky was family. Stinky was going to expect the Meese's *open* and enthusiastic support, no matter who ran against him.

Political campaigns were pretty straight-forward affairs back then. Especially for the lower profile offices. Each candidate printed up some signs with a benign slogan and his picture on it and stuck them on all the telephone poles and empty buildings around town. The candidate might put one of his (no need for using *his or hers* here – no women ran for office in Brookhaven back then) signs in his own yard, and their Mama and Daddy and sisters and brothers might stick one up, but they didn't go around asking for permission to put them in anyone else's yard. It would be too embarrassing to be turned down and everybody knew that nobody wanted to make a bold public commitment to anyone, at least not until after they knew who won. That way everyone could claim to have voted for the winner and nobody could prove they didn't.

The only other way candidates campaigned was to put an ad

in the Brookhaven Leader Times and print up a couple of thousand little business cards to give to everyone they shook hands with or leave at every door they knocked on. Some candidates gave cheap stuff away. Key chains and pencils were popular.

One day Stinky asked Mama and Daddy if he could hire me to give out his cards at the polls on election day. I heard him ask them and I was sure they would say "no" because I knew how they were about politics. Stinky, of course, knew how they were too, but I guess he figured that because we lived next door and used his telephone all the time they couldn't say *no* to him. They were trapped. Stinky asked them and then stood right there waiting for their answer, and I stood right there begging, "please, Mama, please, Daddy, pleeeeeaaasee let me do it." I knew they wished they could get off by themselves and figure out how to get out of making an outright commitment, but they couldn't. They just exchanged looks and kind of shrugged at each other with their eyes. Mama put on her very best smiling company face and told Stinky they would "just love for me to help him get elected," and, "Stinky," she added in the sweet tones she used when praising me, "I'm sure you will make the best tax assessor we ever had."

After Stinky left, Mama started telling Daddy she was sure it was all right for everybody to know we were for Stinky. He was running against a man who never went to church or wore a suit and tie. Besides, she said, he'd never been a customer of ours and, as far as she knew, he didn't have any relatives living in Lincoln County who could get mad and boycott Daddy. Daddy grunted in his ambivalent grunting way. Apparently this *uh huh* meant he agreed with her.

On election day, I stood outside the high school for hours handing a little card and a pencil to everyone going inside, smiled, lowered my pitch and said in my most affectedly professional voice "please vote for Ralph D. "Stinky" Martin." For the most part everyone just took the card, put it in a pocket and kept on going, but one old man who I had never seen before stopped and asked me *why* he should vote for Stinky, what was his *platform*. I didn't know what that meant and I wasn't prepared to answer. I knew Mama and Daddy were voting for Stinky because he lived next door to us and we used his telephone a lot. I figured that wasn't a good enough answer for somebody who didn't live next door to Stinky so I gave him the next best answer I could think of – the honest one.

"Because he's paying me $3.00 to give out his cards," I said. Taken aback by my unexpectedly direct answer, the old man smiled and said, "Well, that's a good enough reason for me."

Later that night, when the results were being hand tallied, we went down to the railroad park. As the votes were counted in City Hall, the Clerk would come across the street and write the numbers down by each candidate's name on a huge blackboard that was set up on the back of a flatbed truck and announce it on a loud speaker to the people gathered around, sitting on the grass, smoking, gossiping and sipping soda pops and bursting into hoops and hollers and whistles when they liked the numbers they saw going up.

Stinky's race for Tax Assessor was never even close. We stayed up at the park for a long time and then Mama and I went home and changed into our night clothes and sat on the top steps. Our apartment was so close, we could hear the returns as the clerk announced them over the loudspeaker. Stinky's early lead kept increasing.

Finally Mama made me go inside and get in bed, but I was so excited I couldn't sleep and I kept calling out in the dark to Mama asking if she was asleep.

"You asleep yet, Mama?"

"No, darlin', not yet.

Then minutes later, "You still awake, Mama?"

After two or three times, she came and sat down beside me. "What's wrong, baby?" she asked, "Can't you sleep?"

"No ma'am. You know why?"

"Why darlin'?"

"'Cause I've been thinking about what I want to be when I grow up."

Most of my life I'd said I wanted to be a teacher, but for the past few months I'd been playing with my chemistry set and trying to invent a new super fertilizer while systematically killing Mama's plants and toying with the idea of growing up to be a famous horticultural scientist.

"I've decided what I *really* want to be when I grow up," I said. "Guess what it is?"

"What?"

"I want to be a Tax Assessor just like Stinky.

Mama quickly bought into my newest pipe dream, patted me and said she was sure that if I wanted to be a Tax Assessor, I would be a great Tax Assessor.

She didn't point out that women didn't run for public office in Brookhaven in the '40s and I, of course, had no idea what a Tax Assessor did. But I'd just had my first taste of politics. And I liked it.

"I've tried and tried but for the life of me, I can't remember the *last* time I fished with Mama or Daddy. I just know that I'll never forget the times in between the first and the last because they were the *best* times of my childhood...."

When I whacked the one in the middle with a window
stick, "She stopped, looked at me in total disbelief, sucked
in all her breath, and held it until she was turning blue."

**"Baby," she said, "this here is lesson #1. In
this world, you either hit or git hit."**

"When Frankie Joe announced that I was his girlfriend, I was pretty sure that this was one of the *somethings* Mama was talking about when she said I could tell her anything."

"I didn't care about Pat running free and procreating
with hound dogs. I didn't want to give my dog
away to anybody, especially since all she was *guilty
of* was loving and trying to protect me."

"Unlike any boy I'd ever seen in Brookhaven, he was
wearing a perfectly white, perfectly starched long-sleeved
dress shirt like Daddy wore with his suit for funerals."

"Since I never in the dozens and dozens of times I went to visit her saw her stand up, put her three hundred plus pounds on her itty bitty feet and walk, I still don't know for sure how Aunt Belle got from one place to another."

"Aunt Edna was the big sister that Mama always looked up to and turned to for help and advice. They told each other everything, and in truth, Aunt Edna really was a model of tee-totaling rectitude."

"When we drove up, Uncle Bud was waiting on the front porch with one of his dogs named Teddy. He always owned at least one dog, and he named every dog he ever had – Teddy. That way he didn't have to remember individual names and when he called Teddy all his dogs came running."

"...the thing I remember most (other than their playing school with me and helping me learn to love learning) was what a *dream enabler* Mama was."

"Mama, of course, raved and raved and called Cat and Irma to brag about her gift. Daddy opened his package and looked at the suit and then looked at me for a long time. Then he mumbled a little thank you, went in the bedroom, took out his handkerchief and wiped his eyes...."

"Because Meese was very old and had arthritis, I'd never seen her move quickly – until the night the squirrels got loose."

"When I started to get up on Slim, he looked back at me with pure mischief in his eyes, almost as if asking, "did you see how I flicked that boy off with no more effort than it takes me to flick flies with my tail?" Then I got on him and he walked back to the pasture as docilely as an old milk cow."

"But she did write back and I was stunned and reduced to tears by her very first words, "Dear Jimmie Lonnie," she began, "of course I remember you. I've prayed for you every day of your life."

Photo credit: The Lincoln Lawrence Franklin
Regional Library, Brookhaven, MS
"When I looked up, I saw my Daddy standing on top of
that firewall holding a hose and shooting water into the
East side of Woolworths, which was engulfed in flames."

My Trip to "It"

I was not by nature a defiant and disobedient child. I tried hard to please my Mama and Daddy and not cause them to worry about me, but one time I ran away from home. About thirteen miles away from home. Now lots of little kids *threaten* to run away from home and some actually do hide in the bushes in their back yard for a few minutes or run around the block and sit down for a few minutes. Most come back when called or when they get hungry or have to go to the bathroom. Not me. When I ran away from home, I made a plan, borrowed some money, bought a ticket, caught a bus and went to "It." It, Mississippi.

Why I ran away from home is not a pretty story. The theme runs skimming through these pages with brief and indirect allusions to my parent's alcoholism. Let's just say I ran away from home at the ripe old age of nine because I wanted to punish them. So one Saturday afternoon I decided to leave them and run away – not just around the block, but far away and It was as far away from Brookhaven as I could figure out how to get.

To implement my plan, I knew I would need money, transportation and a destination. A safe place to go. It filled the bill. It was just a couple of little stores at a crossroads in Copiah County that

132

the Greyhound bus passed on its way to Hazlehurst and points North. When Mama and Daddy were first married they worked for the man who owned the main It Grocery Store and every time Mama and I went to visit Uncle Bud or Aunt Edna, we stopped at It for snacks. And the Crawford home place where my Mama was born was just a couple of miles from It and Uncle Bud and Aunt Myrtis still lived there.

The first thing I did was go to the Greyhound Bus Station and ask the price of a ticket to It.

"Twenty-eight cents," the lady said.

Not much, but a lot more than the nothing I had that day. I decided that I would walk around the block and walk around the block until I saw somebody I knew well enough to go up and ask them to lend me twenty-eight cents. The first time around I saw a lot of folks I knew – but not well enough to ask for a loan. The second time around I saw Sis Lewis coming out of Panzica's Grocery Store. She was a family friend – of sorts. She was a widow and her son Bully was a good customer of ours. I'd been to her house a couple of times.

When I saw Sis that Saturday afternoon, I figured I knew her well enough to ask her for a loan. I went right up to her and without saying so much as "howdy do," I said,

"Miss Sis, I need to borrow twenty-eight cents."

I don't know whether I looked desperate or pitiful or just so earnest she was too startled to ask me any questions.

She just smiled and said, "Sure, Honey" and reached in her purse and got out a quarter and a nickel. Looking back, I probably shouldn't have asked Sis for the loan. She was a widow with no visible means of support and she probably needed that thirty cents more than I did.

"Thank you, ma'am – I'll pay you back," I said and ran all the way back to the bus station, bought a ticket to It and sat in the bus station until the next bus heading North on old highway 51 left. Busses didn't make scheduled stops at It, but if you told the driver you wanted off there, he'd stop and let you. People who wanted to get on the bus just stood out by the road and waved a handkerchief or a rag to flag the bus down.

Mama and Daddy had no idea I'd left Brookhaven and Uncle Bud and Aunt Myrtis had no idea I was on my way to their house.

When I got off the bus, I went in the store and asked if I could use the phone to call Bud Crawford. Mr. and Mrs. Butler, the Mom and Pop of the larger of the two Mom and Pop stores at It didn't seem particularly surprised at seeing a nine year old child from Brookhaven get off the bus, walk in all alone, and ask to use the phone.

Back then, Uncle Bud and Aunt Myrtis were on a party line shared with three other families. Uncle Bud's signal was three short rings, Artie Martin's two longs, Ben Munn's, a short and a long and so on.

Three short rings. No answer. Three short rings again.

It occurred to me that like everybody else out in the country, Uncle Bud and Aunt Myrtis usually went to town to buy groceries on Saturday and I had no idea what I'd do if they weren't at home. I figured that I could just sit out in front of It and flag them down as they came by because they'd have to turn at It to get home and they had to go home to milk the cows. By hand. Uncle Bud and Aunt Myrtis' days always began and ended with pulling cows' tits.

On the third three-ring try, Uncle Bud picked up the phone.

"Yellow!" Uncle Bud always made *hello* sound like *yellow*.

"Hey, Uncle Bud, it's Jim."

"Hey, gal, wha'cha doin'?"

"I'm at It, Uncle Bud. Can you come get me?"

"At It? "What'cha doin' at It, gal?"

Then, "Hey, Myrt, it's Jim. She's at It. You come talk to her."

I could tell Uncle Bud had just realized that he'd never gotten a phone call from his nine-year old niece before, and he knew there was something funny about me, not Mama, calling him. And from It. Not home.

Uncle Bud always handed off to Aunt Myrtis at the first sign of trouble. One, because he really was a simple-minded man. As much a child as an adult, he was not adept at problem solving, and, two, he knew whatever he said or did, Aunt Myrt would over-rule him. Just to be ornery.

Once when the preacher called on Brother Crawford to say a prayer in church, he was so scared that Aunt Myrt might think he didn't pray right that he actually stood up and said, "Preacher, can't you let Myrt do it for me?" so for sure he didn't want to be the one to deal with me being at It on his own.

Aunt Myrtis, who never had children of her own, always adopted the honey-dripping tones and sing songy rhythms of a first grade teacher when she talked to children.

"Hellooo." She also prolonged her vowel sounds.

"Aunt Myrt?"

"Jim?"

"Yes, ma'am."

"Where are you, honey?"

"At It."

"Is Maye with you?"

"No, ma'am."

Long pause. This bombshell only stumped Aunt Myrt for a minute. Then she shifted into her super Myrt mode.

"I'll be right there, honey."

She wasn't about to ask me *why* I was alone at It. She was afraid I might tell her and she knew at that very moment the neighbors were on the party line and Miz Butler was standing right beside me. She worked the party line gossip circle herself, so she didn't *suspect*, she *knew* who else was listening.

When they went to church or to town on Saturday, Aunt Myrt let Uncle Bud do the driving to sustain the illusion that he wore the pants in the Crawford household, but when speed and fine driving skills were required, Aunt Myrt got behind the wheel and attacked Cline Road as if she were on the final lap of a NASCAR race. When Aunt Myrt got to It, she still had on her apron.

You had to hand it to Myrtis Crawford. She tore into It frantic, but hid her anxiety and managed to speak to Miz Butler as calmly as if she came to It in her apron to pick up a run-away child every day.

"Mornin', Miz Butler."

"Mornin', Myrtis."

To me she said something like "so you made it o.k." trying to cover herself by suggesting to Mrs. Butler that she'd been expecting me for a visit and that there was nothing unusual about me riding the bus alone without a suitcase.

When we got in the old Ford, Aunt Myrt ground it into first gear and started creeping down Cline Road as slowly as she could go. She had two miles to get to the bottom of the mystery before she got back to Uncle Bud.

"What's wrong, Jimmie Lonnie?" she asked.

At family reunions at Sylvarena Baptist Church all Mama's country cousins called her Etter Maye, whanging out *Etter*, instead of calling her just plain *Maye*, like everybody in town did. And they all used my middle name and called me Jimmie Lonnie. They all went by double names and figured everybody else ought to be called by every name they had too. But Aunt Myrt had never called me Jimmie Lonnie before. She and Uncle Bud usually called me Jim.

I hesitated for a minute and then said, "I just wanted to come live with you and Uncle Bud."

She clearly hadn't expected that response and it wasn't really true. I loved Mama and Daddy with all my heart and I didn't really want to trade them in for Uncle Bud and Aunt Myrt. For all her sweet dulcet tones, I knew Aunt Myrt was sour at her core. Even when she smiled, the corners of her mouth always turned way down. And I knew that Uncle Bud was simple and weak and couldn't hold a candle to my Daddy. Uncle Bud was the kind of guy that when anyone said his name, always followed it with "bless his heart."

I just told her I wanted to live with them so it would sound like I was running to something good rather than running away from something bad. Besides, I didn't want to have to go in to the whole story and was too loyal to talk bad about Mama and Daddy. Aunt Myrtis knew about Mama and Daddy's drinking and I knew she knew it, but I also knew Mama would never forgive me for talking to anyone about her, especially Aunt Myrtis, who in addition to being sour had a tendency to hold herself up as "holier than" to anyone who didn't go to church as much as she did, which, in her case, was every time they opened the doors at Sylvarena Church. All I wanted was to get Mama and Daddy's attention and get away from them for a little while.

When we drove up, Uncle Bud was waiting on the front porch with one of his dogs named *Teddy*. He always owned at least one dog, and he named every dog he ever had – Teddy. That way he didn't have to remember individual names and when he called *Teddy* all his dogs came running and half the scrawny cats that perpetually waited on the back steps for Aunt Myrt to throw out yesterday's cold biscuits followed them around the corner of the house. They apparently thought they were named Teddy too.

He came off the porch like he always did – firing questions. "What'cha doin'here? Where's Maye? How'd you get up here anyway?" He left no time between questions for answers and when he paused to breathe, Aunt Myrt swooped down on him.

"Hush, Bud!" That was all she said and all she needed to say. Uncle Bud changed course faster than a flock of pigeons in a park.

"Hey, gal, you hungry?" he asked, moving to what he correctly assumed was safer ground. And he knew that I was always hungry when I set foot in their house. We went straight to the kitchen and Aunt Myrt pulled out the breakfast biscuits she'd made at five o'clock that morning. Then she opened the icebox door and got out some wild plum jelly and a chunk of yellow rat cheese.

No more questions were asked. Aunt Myrt left me in the kitchen with Uncle Bud who was still clueless and went to the phone by the fireplace in the front bedroom and called Mama to tell her I was with them and safe and to negotiate the conditions of my return.

I stayed with them for three days and they treated me like I think they thought they would treat their own child. Somehow it seems like childless couples just don't have a knack for acting natural around kids. They were more indulgent this time than they usually were. For the first time ever, they both went with me to the swim hole by the bridge over Bypier Creek. (I always thought Bypier was an odd name for a creek, but that was what everybody called it. So I did too. Many years later I discovered that the creek was actually named Bayou Pierre and correctly pronounced By-yo Pee-yair.) That day I didn't care what it was called. Aunt Myrt gave me one of Uncle Bud's old under shirts to use as a bathing suit, and it got so heavy when it got wet that I thought I'd drown, but it was still fun to be playing in the water and to watch Uncle Bud splashing and teasing Aunt Myrt. She tried to act like she didn't want him messing with her, but she squealed like a teenager when he did.

It was the only time I ever saw Aunt Myrt seem to enjoy what she was doing. She usually acted like everything she did was a duty, and she was damned and determined to do it. She'd make biscuits every morning before daylight and pick tomatoes like a field hand and milk cows when their tits were cold and tend to Bud like he was her child just to prove how dutiful she was. But she did it all with barely concealed misery, so everyone could see what a martyr she was and what a cross she had to bear.

The next day Uncle Bud built me some farm toys like he'd played with when he was a little boy. He showed me how to make a popgun from the hollowed-out stem of a red weed that grew by the barn and some green chinaberries and a stick. When you crammed a chinaberry into each end and used the stick to push one in with a quick thrust, the trapped air between them forced the other one to shoot out like a round green bullet. We also made a play gun from a piece of wood shaped like a real gun. Uncle Bud attached a clothespin to it and cut some rounds of rubber from an old inner tube for ammunition.

Uncle Bud's farm, which all his sisters and brothers, called the "home place" because it was where they were all born had always been a special place for me. It seemed to me that everything I did there was an adventure. Some were exciting; others were sort of spooky.

When Mama and I went for overnight visits to the home place, Aunt Myrtis always got up and made "hotbiscuits" (We never called them just plain biscuits. They were always called *"hotbiscuits"* as if it were one word.) for breakfast and fried some country ham or smoked sausage that they cured themselves in their smokehouse. In the fall, Uncle Bud and Aunt Myrtis and all their neighbors got together when it got cold enough and killed their "hawgs." I never went to a hog-killing. The sight of a chicken killing was enough for me.

After breakfast I went outside and just roamed. I usually picked up a couple of the now cold *hotbiscuits* and headed for the woods at the back of the pasture. There was a little stream bed back there that ran either as a trickle or a torrent, depending on the season.

One of my favorite games out there all by myself was building crawfish cities on moss islands that I built in the middle of the branch. Crawfish, or crawdads, as we called them made perfect little mud-ball mounds that looked just like turrets on fortresses and castles. In the coolest moist crannies around the parts of the interwoven root system that were above ground, green mosses grew. Some were rough to the touch; others soft and fernlike. I'd scoop up chunks of the moss and mound it in the shallow stream to build an island and take crawdad castles and little mushroom umbrellas and put them on the island. Various twigs, acorns, leaves and hickory nut shells became in my imagination boats and cars and stick houses.

To complete my branch world I'd lie down on my stomach and watch the deeper pools for movement until I saw a crawdad scoot backwards along the bottom, then I'd swoop down and rescue "my people" as I called them and put them on my island.

Once when Mama and Daddy left me with Ella May and promised to be home early, but stayed out late drinking, I was so upset and they felt so guilty they promised to buy me a huge set of toy soldiers I'd been asking for. Not the flimsy plastic things they sell now, but heavy metal ones, painted olive green in various poses. With pointed bayonets, kneeling by cannons, holding the flag.

The next time I went to Uncle Bud's after that I took my soldiers with me and staged a big battle between the crawdad people and the metal men. Since the crawdads by their very nature move in perpetual retreat, forever backing up, the green men always won decisively.

I was never afraid down in the pastures by myself, but going in the barn took courage. The big barn, with the hayloft, was all gray wood, dark corners, cobwebs and strange sounds from skittering critters. The perfect place for lizards and rats to scoot about and bats to hang and dangle. I always entered cautiously. What enabled me to confront my fears and climb up into the hay loft was the powerful twin lure of chicken eggs and kittens. Chickens laid eggs up there and cats had their kittens up there.

There was nothing on the farm I loved more than looking for secret hidden chickens' nests. Of course, Uncle Bud and Aunt Myrtis had a regular chicken house, a truly terrifying place for me. It was little more than boards and tin leaning loosely together. Inside it was filled with wooden tomato and cabbage crates filled with straw mounded and rounded by the bodies of the settin' hens. There were a bunch of planks running from one side to the other, up high. Roosting perches. I hated gathering eggs from nests in the chicken house because chicken poop was everywhere and the stench was almost as bad as the inside of their two-hole outhouse in July.

But there were lots of freelancing, independent hens that never deigned to lay an egg in the designated laying place. They made their own decisions and laid eggs all over the farm. Some lazy layin' hens just went over to the edge of the weeds beyond where Uncle Bud mowed. Others went to the back of the garage and the most industrious ones, having made it up to the hayloft, laid their eggs in the fresh hay. I used to try to figure out how they got up there. I guess they flew, though a chicken in flight is an improbable sight. It takes a whole lot of wing flapping to get lift for their big old bodies. I used to laugh to myself trying to imagine a chicken climbing up the ladder to the loft. Once in a while, I'd find a nest crammed full of eggs, a sign – an almost certain sign that many if not all the eggs were rotten, having lain too long undiscovered in the hot Mississippi sun.

The other thing that just absolutely spooked me was when Aunt Myrt killed a chicken for Sunday dinner. I only saw her do it once, but I had nightmares about it for weeks. The first part was funny, watching Aunt Myrt running all over the yard flapping her apron while the fat old hens she was chasing flapped their wings and squawked. When she caught one, she'd hold it by its head and swing it round and round building up centrifugal force. Then she stopped suddenly, made a snapping motion with her wrist and literally pulled its head off, leaving the headless torso flopping around in the yard. Clearly a job for Aunt Myrtis, not Uncle Bud.

Of course, back then I never gave any thought to their division of labor. Now it occurs to me that they actually had a pretty modern marriage. Both did virtually everything together. With two exceptions. Aunt Myrt didn't plow and Uncle Bud didn't cook (at least not until they couldn't earn a living farming any more and Aunt Myrt had to get a job in town.) All other work was shared. They delivered calves and milked cows together, planted, hoed and picked cotton, cabbage and tomatoes together. They washed clothes and ran them through the hand-cranked wringer together.

Aunt Myrtis always made me feel important by letting me help with the chores. In addition to gathering eggs, she'd give me a bucket of corn still on the cob in dried husks to shell into a bucket. The hard, dry corn was rough and hurt my hands. After letting me struggle for awhile, she would come over, pick up two ears and rub them together in a circular motion and make the grains fly off the cob.

I especially loved milking time. Every time I was at the farm when they milked, I just had to try my hand. It looked so easy. All the cows had names and each had a particular stall and knew which one it was. They actually lined up in order outside the barn all by themselves, marched in and headed straight to the right stall. Then Uncle Bud would plop down on his milking stool, grab those big pink tits on their bulging bags and pull until streams of rich milk started flowing as if from a tap, like water. There is no other sound like that of the first stream of milk hitting the bottom of an empty tin bucket. Uncle Bud always pulled the tits smoothly in a steady rhythmic motion, not unlike an orchestra conductor beating out time patterns.

Every once in a while, one of their scrawny cats would sort of tiptoe into the barn, as if trying not to be seen. It would walk right down the center of the aisle in the middle of the barn, steering clear of the cows' hind legs, having either learned from experience or instinctively knew that heifers had a low tolerance for cats getting too close to their tits. Then Uncle Bud would do the most wonderful thing. Without missing a stroke, he could direct a stream of milk from one of the tits straight into the mouth of the waiting cat.

Uncle Bud named the cows with the same originality as he did all his dogs named Teddy. The head cow was always named Pheely, a shortened version of his Mama, Ophelia's name. I won't even speculate on the Freudian implications of his naming all his lead cows for his Mama. The others were named things like Whitey and Blackie and Big and Lit. And he called one of them Dancer because of the way she tapped her foot and swayed from side to side when he milked her.

There was something in the feed room of the milk barn that scared me even more than the hay barn. As soon as each cow poked her head into her stall, she expected someone to get a bucket of oats out of the feed room and put it in her trough. The feed room was a dark, windowless place filled with big fifty pound bags filled with sweet smelling grain – and mice and rats. Opening the door always triggered the sound of scurrying rodents and a rush of motion. As much as I wanted to be the one to fill the bucket and feed the cows, I could never bring myself to touch those bags and dip a bucket down to the bottom. Because of the rodent phobia I caught from my Daddy, I was absolutely positive that if I did a rat would touch my hand and I would die right then and there.

One summer I wound up getting to pick tomatoes with Uncle Bud and Aunt Myrt and their sharecroppers and I loved it. There is something inexplicably, yet intrinsically beautiful about seeing a field of ripening tomatoes. Some people's *hearts leap up when they behold a rainbow in the sky;* mine leaps up when I behold a ripe red tomato on a green tomato vine.

At one time, a family of sharecroppers lived in a shack next to Uncle Bud's house. Clare Harvey, the matriarch of the clan, lived there with her daughters Crow and Yella. When Mama was a baby, Clare Harvey was her wet nurse. Mama was the youngest child in a family of twelve, so by the time she was born, Pheely

Crawford was pretty well drained – so to speak – and Clare Harvey nursed her babies for her.

Clare Harvey was a long, tall angular very very black woman, rail thin with graying hair twisted into a dozen short braids. She was by most accounts the fastest cotton and tomato picker in Copiah County. She could have gotten work on anybody's farm, but she said that the Crawford home place was her home place too, and no matter how hard they tried, Crow and Yella never could get her to move.

Aunt Myrt and Uncle Bud were the only white people inside the sweltering AME Tabernacle Church for Clare Harvey's funeral. Aunt Myrt said Crow and Yella wailed and moaned when the choir sang "In the Sweet By and By" and clung to the casket all the way to the hole in the ground in the cemetery behind the church, crying,

"Oh Lord, Mama, what we gonna do without you?"

By the time I ran away to It, Yella and Crow had moved away and the falling down old shack they had been born in had finally fallen all the way down. The last time I looked, there was no sign that there had ever been a house there where people lived and shelled field peas and made cornbread and washed clothes in a big black pot in the yard. And prayed and nursed other folks' babies.

I had one of the most memorable experiences of my childhood walking down the road in front of Clare Harvey's house. The road was gravel and hard to walk on barefooted, but on the side of the road there were mounds of dirt so fine it felt like talcum powder beneath my feet, much softer than the finest sand at the beach. One day when I was picking blackberries from the side of the road for Aunt Myrt to make a cobbler, I consciously pressed my feet into that warm dirt and dragged them through it so it got between my toes and it felt so good and soothing that I had my first known epiphany of self-awareness. I was in the middle of experiencing one of the most utterly special sensory pleasures

I'd ever known and I was aware of it in a curiously objective and detached way.

I stopped and just let myself enjoy the feel of the warm powder on my feet and thought to myself "this is what childhood is all about. I don't think Mama and Daddy or any adult would ever understand what I am feeling. I want to remember this day, this place and this feeling for the rest of my life. Mark it in your mind. Don't forget it." And I haven't. Every time I drive by to look at the old home place and pass that spot on the road, I remember. I think it is the only memory that I had the presence to make a conscious effort to capture. I wish I had done it more.

The "Crawford home place" was always a safe haven for me as a child. No wonder that when I ran away to punish my parents, I went to the "home place."

Mama and Daddy let me stay at the farm for three days when I ran away to It and then Mama drove up to get me. As always, she wanted to avoid talking about what happened. "Let's just bury the hatchet," she said which is what she always said when she didn't want to confront the consequences of her drinking, but she didn't drink again for almost a year.

Some fifty years later, Uncle Bud and Aunt Myrtis left that safe "home place" and ten acres of land to me in their will.

Softly and Tenderly Jesus Is Calling

*L*ong before I was immersed in the lighted waters of the Baptismal pool above and behind the pulpit of the First Baptist Church, I was immersed in the rhythms of the church. I got my first Perfect Attendance Award before I was good and potty-trained because Mama toted me to Sunday school every single Sunday for a year.

Sunday after Sunday, year after year, I went and listened to Brother Miller, our regular preacher, and resisted every one of his soft seductive post-sermon calls to give my soul to Jesus.

When I was twelve, a traveling tent revival evangelist came to town and Mama and I went to every service. I sat there night after night listening to fiery flamboyant threats of hellfire and brimstone and impassioned invitations to be born again and take Jesus as my personal savior. I still resisted. I was stirred inside. I believed. And as I tried to be a perfect child for Mama and Daddy, I also wanted to do the right thing by my Father in Heaven, but every time I started to stand up for Jesus, something inside held me back.

After every sermon Brother Miller would come down from the pulpit, stand in the front of the sanctuary and do a kind of

Price is Right announcer's call to "Come on down." As the music played and we bowed our heads and the choir sang, Brother Miller kept softly and tenderly and piously imploring us to "come on down."

But it wasn't the evangelist's fiery sermons or Brother Miller's sweet calls that finally got me. It was the music. The affective power of *"softly and tenderly Jesus is calling... calling to you and to me...come home... come home... ye who are weary come home – ohm ohm"* finally moved me beyond resistance.

One Sunday morning I watched as a couple of sinners went down the aisle, grabbed Brother Miller's out stretched palms and promised their souls to Jesus. As the choir repeated the chorus over and over and over – softly – and tenderly, I was moved so deeply and truly by the emotional impact of the music and my own growing sense of need for personal redemption that I finally gave up, walked down the aisle, surrendered all and joined the soon to be re-born in the front of the church.

Finally Aunt Edna could relax. I had been turned into – not a Roman Catholic – but one of God's favored Baptist children.

Brother Miller sealed the deal a few weeks later. I donned a white robe and waded over to the middle of the Baptismal pool where Brother Miller took the handkerchief I proffered, put it over my nose and slid me backward and under the water that would wash away my twelve years of backlogged sin – slid me all the way under the water – a la John the Baptist. None of that trickle on the forehead business for us Baptists. We went all the way under.

When I waked up Monday morning the day after I was saved, I lay in bed for a while thinking about what being born again felt like and wondering if the cleaning immersion had made any changes that I could see. Did I look happier or feel purer? Apparently not. When I got up and stared at myself in the mirror, the same scrawny little girl with big brown eyes was staring back at me. Only now I was redeemed!

147

The summer after I was saved we went to visit Aunt Bess and Uncle Wamon in Houston, Texas, again. I really despised Wamon Davis, for more reasons than I could count. For starters, he was a holier than thou "Holy Roller" and a first-rate hypocrite. His false teeth didn't fit right and he made a smushy sound and spewed spittle when he talked. When he said the blessing, he prayed so long the food got cold. When I was badly sun-burned, he slapped me on my back and grinned. When I went to the movie with Harold Fisher, he teased me in a sing-songy "nanny nanny boo boo" kind of way. He thought he was funny and he wasn't. Most of all I couldn't stand him because every time I saw him when a hug was in order, he always tried to kiss me on my mouth. And nobody in my family kissed each other on the mouth.

Every time we went to Houston, he tried to get all of us to go to church with him. Mama always made some kind of excuse. Daddy just ignored him. But this time, in spite of my known aversion to him, when he invited us to go, Mama declined but said I should go to church with him.

Uncle Wamon's church was like no other church I'd ever been to before. When I said he was a "Holy Roller" I used the term not pejoratively, but descriptively. I just didn't know what Holy Roller meant until the Sunday I went to church with Uncle Wamon. It was a pretty enough church. And large. The worshippers looked pretty much like worshippers every where, except there was no color anywhere. Everyone was in black or gray or navy. All the women's dress sleeves were long. And nobody smiled. It was clear from the git-go that these people were serious about their God stuff.

The preacher, an old man who looked a little bit like Abraham Lincoln, began with a long, long, long prayer. Then he started reading the Bible, and he read and read and read. I was tired and sleepy and ready to go home before he started preaching. When he did start, he started slowly enough, but pretty soon started talking really loud and really fast, and when he did all of a sudden people began shouting "Amen," "Yes, Lord," "Hallelujah," and the like. Then a woman stood up and started moaning and making sounds in an untranslatable language. She waved her arms and rolled her eyes and babbled for a long time and then she just collapsed like she had fainted. All the while the Preacher kept on preaching and the congregation got more and more frenzied and other people hopped up and started doing the same thing. I guess because I was with him, Uncle Wamon just sat beside me. His eyes were fixed like he was in a trance – but he didn't get up and shout. I couldn't make out much of what the preacher was saying, but every once in while he would say something about the walls of Jericho.

When he got to the end of the sermon, he asked everybody to march around the walls of Jericho and everybody stood up, got in a single file line and started marching around and around the sanctuary. While Uncle Wamon had resisted talking in tongues, he jumped up and got in line to march around the walls of Jericho and I went with him.

When we got back to Aunt Bess's, Mama took me off to the side and asked me how it was and I was speechless. Didn't know where to begin. I just made a face and shrugged, but the next time I went to my own church, I appreciated Brother Miller's restraint a whole lot more.

While that was by far the strangest experience I ever had in a church, over time my personal theological journey took many turns. In college I believed for a while that I was called to be a Baptist missionary. As a debate coach I became disillusioned with the insularity of the Baptist church and for awhile my rational analytical impulses overwhelmed my emotions and I left the Baptist church and searched for years for a new church home. I talked to Sister Clare about Catholicism and Mormon neighbors about their faith. I married a man whose life was formidably shaped by the Episcopal Church and seven years later I was confirmed in that faith.

Then I just stopped going to church for a long time. I didn't stop believing – I just didn't want to get up, get dressed and leave the house on Sunday morning.

Now I am a member of a Presbyterian Church. Comfortable in my church home.

People have asked me what Presbyterians believe. I tell them I don't really know what Presbyterians believe or Baptists or Episcopalians for that matter. I only know what I believe.

From my Baptist-Episcopal-Presbyterian perspective I have concluded that Baptists have the best hymns and singers, Episcopalians have the prettiest churches, and Presbyterians probably do the best job of "doing unto others as they would have others do unto them."

First Date

Mama and Daddy and I didn't ever as long as they lived take a real vacation where you went and stayed in a motel at a beach or in the mountains or in a city where none of your relatives lived. We went to Aunt Bess and Uncle Wamon's house in Houston, Texas, a couple of times, and once to Daddy's Aunt Ellie's in Illinois, but we got there at night after she had gone to bed and she died before morning, so we stayed for her funeral; then drove back home and never went to Illinois again.

Aunt Bess didn't have any children to play with me, so when we went to her little house on Wipprecht Street, I just sat around and watched all the adults, except Uncle Wamon, drink. We didn't do any sight seeing to speak of, except once we drove out to see the San Jacinto Monument and the Battleship Texas, and I was disappointed with them. I didn't know what kind of sights other people saw when they went on real vacations and went sightseeing. I guess I expected something more like a National Geographic moment.

Another time we went out to some river to go swimming and have a picnic. This sounded exciting, like something other people might do on a real vacation. But it wasn't. As it turned out, on hot

July days just about everybody in Houston went to a river. Instead of a quiet, cool, sweet-smelling river like the creeks in Lincoln County, we scrambled around for a long time competing with a slew of other cursing, frustrated drivers looking for a place to park, and when we finally found one, we got out of the car and walked into a zoo.

Most of the adults were either already drunk and loudmouthed or trying to get there. Their kids were loud, hyper and intimidating. And the river was, in the middle of the summer drought season, little more than a knee-deep mud-hole. I spent the whole time walking up and down the banks of the river, moving slowly, with my head down, staring at the water, searching for any of the stirring and rippling signs that fish make. Then we ate some pimento cheese sandwiches and fried chicken and potato salad and went back to Aunt Bess' house.

While trips to Houston never qualified as a real vacation, one visit was notable for another reason. I met Harold Fisher there when I was twelve. Until then I never ever felt pretty. I was a gawky kid and like Pig Pen Patty always unkempt with skinned and scabby knees. I couldn't imagine that any boy, especially a cute one, would like me, but Harold Fisher did.

The first time I saw him he was leading his horse down the street and stopped in front of Aunt Bess' to let Trigger drink from the standing water in the ditch in front of her house. Back then all children who were lucky enough to have their own horse named it Trigger – especially if it were a palomino like Roy Rogers' super horse and movie legend of the same name.

I'd gotten tired of hitting a croquet ball through little wickets all morning and was sitting in the swing glider out under Aunt Bess' weeping willow tree when Harold and his Trigger came by. I was transfixed. I hardly noticed Harold at first, but I couldn't take my eyes off of his horse. He was the horse I had dreamed about all my life.

Turned out that Harold lived only a couple of blocks away

and his Mama was a friend of Aunt Bess'. I was so clearly excited about seeing the horse and so generally bored and tired of hitting croquet balls by myself that Aunt Bess called Mrs. Fisher and maneuvered the conversation around until she got Mrs. Fisher to invite me over to visit with Harold and his horse.

Aunt Bess walked me down, talked to Mrs. Fisher for a while and left me there. With typical twelve-year old girl meets thirteen-year old boy timidity, when Harold and I were left alone we just stared at each other awkwardly for a little while, uncertain what to say or do. He finally managed to ask if I had a horse and I said no. Then for the first time, I took a really good look at Harold and realized in my first breathtaking "puppy-love-*aha*-moment" that Harold Fisher was cute. Really cute and he was a boy and he was talking to me as normally as if I were another thirteen year old boy or a *pretty* girl.

Harold had three things I never had and would never have: curly hair, a perfect little turned-up button nose, and on that perfect little turned-up button nose, a perfect little sprinkling of perfect little freckles. Harold was gorgeous and different. Unlike any boy I'd ever seen in Brookhaven, Harold was wearing a perfectly white, perfectly starched long-sleeved dress shirt like Daddy wore with suits for funerals. He had on blue jeans, but they'd been starched stiff and ironed with a sharp crease down the front of the pants legs.

I stayed at Harold's house all afternoon. We rode Trigger separately and then together – at the same time – which required actually touching each other. Another first for me. Then we went inside for awhile and I realized that I was truly smitten when we played checkers and I didn't even try to beat him, though I still had all the checker-whiz skills I'd learned playing with all the old men at the fire station when Daddy was a fireman.

Harold and I hit it off so well that Mama let me ask him to go on our sightseeing trip to the San Jacinto Monument. Somewhere I have pictures of me sitting awkwardly by Harold Fisher at the base of a monument and another of me leaning on a big gun on a battleship. In both, I was wilted and rumpled and Harold was perfect in his cool crisp long sleeved white shirt.

I guess it was pretty clear to all the adults that Harold and I really liked each other, because they started doing what insensitive adults do to children everywhere. They started teasing us. Not when we were together. Most of them weren't that mean, except Uncle Wamon, the Crude. He tormented me with a sing-songy chant, "nanny nanny boo boo...Jimmie has a boyfriend kind of chant." Though it was true, it still made me mad and I kept on denying it until my first date.

Harold Fisher asked me if I would like to go to a movie! I couldn't believe it. He was suggesting that he and I go somewhere together – alone. By anyone's definition, this was a date. My first date.

When he asked me to go to a movie, he didn't "hem and haw" or anything. He just came right out and said the words, "Would you like to go to a movie with me?" Just him and me.

His Mama and Daddy and my Mama and Daddy and Aunt Bess all agreed. Ms. Fisher drove us over to a little movie theater, let us out, gave Harold some money and drove away. Harold bought my ticket and some popcorn and a coca-cola and some candy and he held the door open for me when we went in. You'd think I would remember what was playing that day, but I don't. I just sat there, looking at the beautiful boy beside me with his curly hair and perfect button nose and freckles.

Then – here comes the truly unbelievable part – when the movie was over, Harold called a taxi cab and we rode home all by ourselves like grown-ups. I kept a little diary then and filled my account of that day with !!!!!!!!!! s. I'd had my first date and my first taxi ride. All on the same day.

And if that wasn't enough to qualify as a real vacation, I also met my first real live American Indian on that trip. Leon Mouton. He looked a whole lot like the guy on the buffalo nickel and he was reddish brown and he talked with an accent not unlike the Indians in the Roy Rogers and Gene Autry movies. I tried to get him to go "<u>Wah</u> wah wah wah...<u>wah</u> wah wah wah" the way Indians beat drums and chanted in the movies, but he just laughed.

Leon was, as my Uncle Bud would say, "made funny." He was short and walked bent over and twisted around to one side, and he had to keep his neck bent back so he could hold his head up enough to look at you and talk to you. His arms and legs and neck were real skinny, but he had an unnaturally huge protruding belly that pulled him forward and killed him. Literally. He died not too long after we got back to Mississippi. Aunt Bess wrote Mama and told her that the thing in his belly was a cancer "big as a watermelon" that just ate him up. Said they cut him open, looked inside, and sewed him right back up to die. And he did.

By the next time we went back to Houston, the Fishers had moved. Through mutual friends, Aunt Bess kept up with Miz Fisher for a long time. Last I heard, Harold Fisher had quit school and was driving a truck.

The Night Big Daddy Slept in the Little Bed

_W_hile all _firsts_ have the potential to live long in our memories, not all _firsts_ are of joyous and exciting experiences.
I also vividly remember something about my first experience
with death.

I don't remember a whole lot about my grandparents. Two of
them died before I was born – Daddy's Daddy, Joseph Lafayette
Meese, and Mama's Mama, Ophelia Case Crawford. My sustained
memories of Daddy's Mama, Glendora Judd Meese, a quiet, soft-
spoken Quaker woman don't begin until she was already in the
throes of senile dementia.

I don't remember a whole lot about Mama's Daddy, Quincy
Gardner Crawford, either, but the two memories I do have are
extraordinarily vivid and unforgettable.

One day Big Daddy was sitting out on the top step of our
back porch smoking a cigar and I was sitting beside him. He
was blowing perfect smoke rings for me – one right after the
other. I called what he was doing "hoppin." I have no idea why I
called it hoppin', any more than I know why I called egg beaters
"zigzags." I was sitting right beside him holding a little pickling
cucumber, putting it in my mouth and pretending to puff and

156

blow smoke rings too. When Mama came out on the porch to see what we were doing, I looked up at her, sucked on the cucumber, pretended to blow a smoke ring and said, "Look, Mama, I can hop like Big Daddy." That's it. Just one little slice of what would seem to be a pedestrian and wholly forgettable experience. But it is the only memory I have of my Big Daddy – alive, and I treasure it along with the fading black and white photographs I have of him.

My first memory of death came not long after Big Daddy and I sat on our back porch and "hopped" together. Big Daddy died. Back then the body of the deceased was sometimes taken in the casket back to the home of a family member for the wake, instead of holding the wake at the funeral home. Big Daddy's body was taken to Aunt Edna's house in Hazlehurst so friends and relatives could come by, view the corpse, offer words of love and consolation and eat - fried chicken, potato salad, pimento cheese sandwiches, pound cake, and the ubiquitous deviled eggs, the culinary staple of all Southern family reunions, picnics and funerals.

The men, uncomfortable in the neckties their wives made them wear, also used wakes as a time for getting together outside to smoke and chew and tell jokes and lie, and occasionally, if they remembered why they were there, to mumble something respectful about the deceased. This was a difficult exercise for that generation of silent men. Spontaneous eulogizing was not their forte. For their dead men friends, the most common pro-nouncement went something like, "By God, I tell you what, son, Old Quinn was a good man. He'd give you the shirt right off his back." For some reason, the ultimate test of *goodness* lay in the willingness to give away your shirt. To show respect for women, the men could usually find no higher praise than to compliment her cooking. "I'm telling you that woman could cook red-eye gravy! I mean, she could make a biscuit that would float off your plate."

When Mama and I got to Aunt Edna's, everybody was red-eyed and crying and whispering and hugging and patting each other. All her cousins swooped down on Mama when we walked in, offering her hugs and comfort. Usually when something bad happened or somebody died, Aunt Edna would tell Mama, "It's all for the best, darlin'. Everything happens for the best, Maye." When she said that to Mama that night, Mama started crying uncontrollably.

Mama carried me into the dining room where the casket stood open between the two windows of the outer side wall of the room so I could see Big Daddy. She didn't say anything to me about death. She just held me and stood there and looked at her dead Daddy and cried.

After we stared at Big Daddy for a while, Mama took me down the hall to Aunt Edna and Uncle Pap's bedroom at the back of the house, put me in their big bed and told me we were going to spend the night with Aunt Edna.

Then Mama said I started crying and crying and when she sat down on the bed beside me and started trying to soothe and comfort me, I said, "Why are y'all making Big Daddy sleep in that little bed?"

It just didn't seem right that I got to sleep in a great big bed all by myself while big old Big Daddy slept in that little bitty bed in the dining room. My first experience with death didn't seem frightening so much as it just seemed *unfair*.

Shooting Stars and Sunset Carson

Most of the "exciting" things I remember doing as a child seem decidedly pedestrian now, but back then the bar for measuring excitement was considerably lower. In a small town in Mississippi in the 40s, a town over which the First Baptist Church loomed large, excitement and adventure, such as they were, were tinged by an innocence and naiveté.

Now I get excited about things like a new production of Cirque Du Soleil, a laser show on the side of Stone Mountain, hitting three red sevens on a dollar slot machine, catching a thirty-pound rooster fish in Costa Rica, or riding an elephant in Northern Thailand, but when I lived in "Homeseeker's Paradise" small simple pleasures were just as grand.

I got excited at Christmas when the grocery stores stocked up on citrus fruits and carried kumquats. I got excited around the 4th of July when we went to the fireworks stand and bought all the "safe" stuff – stuff that could blow your fingers off, but probably wouldn't kill you. I got excited walking with Daddy through fields beside creeks to look for honey hole fishing spots. I got really excited when Daddy paid somebody to fly him and me over Brookhaven in an airplane about the size of our bathtub, and I will certainly never forget how excited I and everybody else in Lincoln County got at seeing our first television set. Before anybody I knew actually owned one, the Western Auto Store put one in their front display window and left it on at night for a couple of weeks.

When word spread to the dairy farms and trailer parks and country stores out in Lincoln County about the box with the flickering pictures in the window at the Western Auto Store, farmers, pine-resin-reeking pulp wood haulers, cotton pickers and others too old or lazy to do anything more than sit on porches started coming into town after dark on weekdays.

The pull of the pictures-in-a-box attraction was so great that it actually countered well-established mobility patterns among rural Lincoln Countians. Under normal circumstances, people from out in the county only came to town during the day and then mostly on Saturday to buy groceries, kids'clothes, gasoline and such. Weekday visits were made only of necessity – to see their doctor, go to the funeral home, or worse still, to go to a lawyer or the bank. Seeing a lawyer meant you were in some kind of real trouble and going to the bank was even worse. Most of the county people didn't have a bank account because they didn't have any money to put in one and they wouldn't have put it in the bank if they had had any because they had lived through the depression and were afraid to put their money any place where they couldn't see it. And showing up at the bank with hat in hand to ask a man in a suit with clean fingernails to lend you money was torturous and demeaning and usually resulted in failure.

Of course there were some exceptions. There were times when just about everybody came to town. Everybody came to town when the real Ringling Brothers-Barnum and Bailey Circus off-loaded their exotic pleasures in the pasture just south of the Big Coffee Pot, a truck stop café distinguished only by the friendliness of its waitresses and the signature twenty-foot tall coffeepot that sat on its roof. When the circus came to town, everybody lined the streets to watch some weary-looking weathered old elephants hold tails and lumber down Main Street while a real calliope tootled and thundered marches with rhythms so irresistible that you just had to pat your foot and jiggle your hips. Even the most reticent and repressed old Episcopalians, who had never "dared to eat a peach" in their lives, sneaked in a head bob or two now and then and snapped their fingers behind their backs to the pumping of the pipes.

Lots of folks came to town the time an ICRR train off-loaded a car on a side rail over by the packing shed with a big banner on the side that announced the arrival of a "Jonah Whale: The World's Largest Sea Monster." Some enterprising showman had bought a beached whale down in Florida, had it stuffed and was hauling it up and down the ICRR path from New Orleans to Chicago, stopping for a few days in the small adventure-starved towns that lined the tracks. For ten cents you could walk through that railroad car and stay as long as you could stand to stay in there looking at a big dead whale. But since there were lingering vestiges of the smell of the sea and blubber emanating from the whale, most people just handed the man a dime and went through as fast as they could.

Daddy, of course, didn't go anywhere, except fishing, but I think he was really tempted to go see the "big fish." Mama, who usually humored me and gave in to all my pleas, for some reason refused to go to the whale exhibit with me. So I went by myself. Understand, doing things and going places by myself wasn't all that unusual. I went all over town by myself all the time. I rode my bicycle down through the quarters collecting bills for Daddy. I even went to the dentist by myself.

It wasn't a bad thing. It was just that *by myself* was the way I preferred doing a lot of things and, being the only child of alcoholic parents it was the way I *had to do* a lot of things.

The only thing I remember that I couldn't handle by myself was getting a hot perm at the May Sisters Beauty Parlor. My hair was a problem from the day I was born. I was born bald-headed and stayed that way until I was almost two years old and had long legs and knobby knees. When I did finally get a little bit of hair, it was straight and fine as silk. Bless her heart though, Mama was determined that her baby was gonna have curly hair even if she had to glue it in place, so when I was about four or five years old she started rolling my hair every Saturday night in something she called dipsy doodle curlers, which were pieces of leather with a slit in one end to pull the other end through. Somehow Mama managed to wrap those things around the fuzz on my head and twist and pull it hard enough to make my eyes water. No matter how much I wiggled and yowled and begged for mercy, Mama was relentless. She didn't stop until every little hair was pulled, twisted, and bound, and as bad as it hurt when she was twisting it, the pain didn't end when she stopped, because I still had to go to bed and sleep with those dipsy doodles in my hair.

When I got a little older, Mama decided that I needed to have a more permanent solution and started giving me home perms. She bought the ones that were just supposed to make soft waves in hair, but there was no way to make soft waves in my thin limp fuzz, so the perms Mama gave me ended up making my hair so dried out and curly that I always wound up with a tangled mass of fried tight uncombable kinky curls. Mama's home waves also had a way of turning my hair orange, so she finally gave up and decided to stop torturing me herself and send me to a real beauty parlor to let a professional do it for her.

She decided I needed to have a *hot* perm. Now, getting a *hot* perm involved rolling the hair around huge heavy metal rollers and then taking some thing-a-ma-bobs that looked like big steel clothes pins that were hanging down on electric wires, hooking them over the round rollers and turning on the current.

Not realizing that I was in store for a near-death experience, I assured Mama that I was a big girl and she didn't need to walk me to the beauty parlor and wait for me. I could do it by myself.

I was wrong. As it turned out I wasn't nearly a big enough girl to get a *hot* wave all by myself. I sat through the rolling part without a problem, chatting with the oldest May sister about their mayhaw trees. The May sisters had a grove of May haws on their farm and I'd been out to there a couple of times with Mama and Daddy to get some for Mama to make jelly.

When the oldest May sister finished yanking me around and rolling me, she motioned for me to follow her and started walking toward a machine that took my breath away. It looked like a cross between what I imagined the electric chair to look like and a torture machine I had seen in a Saturday movie serial in a cave where a half-man, half-lizard monster captured his victims to be guinea pigs for his mad master's scientific experiments. It also looked a little bit like an octopus – only the tentacles were big thick electric wires like the cords on Mama's iron. All of a sudden, when I began to imagine just how hot that hot perm was going to be, I balked.

All the May sisters were old maids, the really plain homely kind of old maids, and I always thought it was strange that they spent most of their lives making other women look pretty, while they apparently gave absolutely no thought to how they looked. Unlike most of the salon hair people I see now who use each other for guinea pigs and try to out do each other seeing how outrageous they can make human hair look, the May sisters all had straight bowl cut haircuts, utterly devoid of style. They also had no sense of humor and as it turned out no patience with recalcitrant children, so when I balked, the oldest May sister smiled at me condescendingly and decided she'd just pull me over to "the chair." When she grabbed my arm, I sat down, dragged my rubber-heeled shoes across the floor and declined to be electrocuted as politely as I could under the circumstances. Of course, all the women in the shop stopped gossiping for a minute, put their movie magazines in their laps and giggled nervously. Normally I would have been embarrassed about causing such a commotion in public. But this time I really didn't care. I knew that resisting an adult, especially one you weren't related to was impolite, and possibly even illegal, but I really did not want that woman hooking me up to that machine.

Under the scrutiny of all her customers, the oldest May sister, changed tactics. She let go my arm and tried to reason with me by assuring me that her customer-hot-perm survival rate was 100%. I didn't move. She offered me some hard candy as a bribe, and tried to embarrass me by suggesting I was just a big baby, but I still wouldn't get up.

It was clear that we were at an impasse. I had her rollers in my hair and she was determined that, by God, she was gonna finish her job. I was equally determined not to let her electrocute me without my Mama, so I suggested a compromise. I told her I would sit under her machine if she would let me go home and get my Mama. She agreed.

Even as good a pro as the oldest May sister was, it had taken her a long time to twist my soft hair around those iron rods, and she wasn't about to take the curlers down and do it all over again. She insisted that I leave the rods in, and she put a big hair net over my head. I left the shop and walked down Main Street with my head wobbling and bobbing under the weight of the rollers and at the same time, tried to act as if there were nothing unusual about my appearance. When I passed Miss Ella Lee, our next door neighbor, coming out of Janie's Bakery, she stared at me – rather impolitely, I thought, but I just nodded my head and said, "Morning, Miz Lee." It was, of course, a mistake to try to nod my head, because when I did it just kind of rolled over on my shoulder, but I kept on walking.

Mama was surprised when she heard me coming back in and gasped when she got a good look at me. She couldn't imagine what I was doing back so soon and with permanent paraphernalia all over my head. I started talking real fast the way I always did when I was trying to tell Mama something embarrassing, incriminating, or that I thought might make her nervous. I blurted out that I had just had a near death experience, that the oldest May sister had tried to electrocute me and that I needed her – really needed her with me. She, of course, agreed that no child should have to risk electrocution at the beauty parlor without her Mama and went back to the shop with me where the oldest May sister fried my hair to her satisfaction without further delay.

I've always identified with that guy in the Edgar Alan Poe story who had a heightened sense of hearing because I've always been convinced that I have a heightened and unusually refined sense of smell. Once when Mama and I went to Dallas to visit Uncle Hebo and his second wife, Gladys, I nearly embarrassed Mama to death. I thought their dark old apartment smelled like somebody had been cooking cheap hamburger meat, and I thought Gladys needed to wash and comb her hair and take a bath so I held my breath as much as I could and stayed outside on the porch as much as I could, because I absolutely refused to eat anything that Gladys cooked.

When the big whale came to town, I was torn. On one hand, I considered myself one of the more worldly children in Brookhaven, having pretty much absorbed everything my *World Book Encyclopedias* had to offer. I was determined to broaden my horizons by taking advantage of every cultural opportunity that presented itself – whether it came to town in the form of a stuffed whale or rodeo cowboys.

On the other hand, I suffered from this heightened sense of smell that made it possible for me to engage in certain activities only for as long as I could hold my breath. Forewarned at school that the whale was really stinky, I decided to use preemptive measures to block the bad smell by dousing myself with good smells. My favorite scents then were gardenias, cinnamon, and Mama's special smell, which was a mixture of her Coty's face powder, Evening in Paris Perfume and Jergen's Lotion. I dabbed a little of her stuff on my wrists and ears, and then dabbed a little more, and for good measure dabbed a little more. Then I stuck a red bandana that I used in cowboy games in my pocket in case I needed a mask.

The whale car was parked on a side rail up by the packing shed where when crops were in season, farmers brought and sold wooden crates of tomatoes and cabbage and corn and watermelons and where one of the Case brothers sold fireworks for the 4th of July and New Year's Eve.

When I realized that I had overdone it with the good smells, and with the memory of traipsing through town with iron curlers in my hair still fresh in mind, I decided not to walk through town to see the Jonah whale. Instead, I got on my bike and cut through the railroad park. When I got to the little flimsy outhouse kind of booth where a man with really greasy hair was selling tickets I remembered that I didn't have any money, so I turned around and headed to the service station to get a dime from Mama.

I guess I worked up a bit of a sweat riding my bike, and apparently the heat and sweat were perfect catalysts for intensifying the blended smells of perfume, powder and hand lotion. By the time I got to the station, I reeked. I'd hoped Mama would be alone at the cash register because I knew that she would pretend she didn't notice anything unusual. Mama was genuinely understanding and kind about things like that, but when I got to the station, Troy Cowart was sitting in there with her. (Daddy loved homemade hominy and Troy cooked up a batch of it every year in a big black iron pot in his yard and had brought a bucketful to Daddy.) I knew if I went inside, Troy would tease me about the way I smelled and I hated being teased, so instead of going inside the station, I motioned to Mama through the station window to come outside. When she came out and started toward me, I tried to back away from her, but she still got close enough to me to get a good whiff and didn't even ask why I had called her outside.

"Mama," I said, "I need a dime to go see the whale."

Without a word, she went back in and got me a dime out of the cash register, and as she handed it to me, she smiled her beautiful "good Mama" smile – the one that always made me feel good and she hugged me. Then she looked at me the way Mamas do when they know just what you need to hear them say and said, "My my, baby, you sure do smell good." I got back on my bike and rode off to see the whale, and I loved my Mama so much I thought I would bust.

As it turned out, the boys at school had told the truth. The Jonah whale was huge and smelled way worse than Paul's Fish Market. Until then, the biggest fish I had ever seen was a catfish that Uncle Ed had "tickled" (hand grabbed) out of a log in a hole in the bank of Pearl River. It had weighed close to forty pounds, and this whale weighed thousands of pounds – or so the sign claimed. I held my breath and stared at it as long as I could. I was pretty sure that nothing in life could be more exciting than seeing a really big dead fish.

And that was true until the rodeo came to town. Out on the east side of Brookhaven, close to where Ella May lived, some local entrepreneur cleared off an acre or two, built some fences and chutes and bleachers and hooked up with a traveling show that brought bulls and horses and clowns and grade B movie cowboy stars to town for a rodeo. For four consecutive years, rodeo week brought some real, raw excitement to town – and celluloid cowboys. One year Sunset Carson came. The next year, Lash Larue. Then Don Red Barry, and finally Tim Holt, whose autograph I managed to get when a crowd gathered at the railroad station just to watch him get off the train. Don Red Barry must have been impressed with what he saw, because a few years later he came back and made a movie on location out near Silver Creek. It was called "Jesse James' Women" and one of Booty Brueck's sisters who had won a local beauty contest had a starring role.

For pure excitement, Brookhaven had never seen anything like the rodeo. It had a little bit of everything – calf roping, barrel racing, bull-riding, clowns in barrels, falls and tumbles and bowlegged cowboys wearing rhinestones and chaps – sometimes strutting around proudly and other times running for their lives a few steps ahead of a bull's horns, scrambling to get back to the chute fence hoping the clowns in the barrels could divert the bull's attention and literally save their butts.

Underscoring how real and dangerous a rodeo could be, an ambulance was always parked behind the bleachers, but I never heard of anybody getting hurt bad enough to get hauled off in it.

You'd think those bull and bronco riders would break every bone in their body when they fell off. But they didn't. They just bounced when they hit the ground and hopped up and hobbled off.

The prettiest part of the whole thing was the opening parade. That was when all the cowboys rode in on their beautiful palominos and pintos and black stallions while they were all still clean before they got thrown and messed up their sparkling pearl-buttoned shirts. After all the real cowboys were in and circling the arena, there was a big drum roll, the music crescendoed, the gates swung open and the celluloid cowboy star came tearing in on the prettiest horse of all, raced all the way around the arena a time or two, then went to the center of the ring, raised his hat in the air, nodded his head and smiled and flashed his perfect white teeth while the crowd roared its approval.

I don't know why, but after the fourth year, the rodeo never came back to town again. It didn't take very long at all for the bleachers to weather and rot and crumble. A few years later, East Haven Baptist Church bought the property and built a nice brick church and a big cemetery on the very spot where the cowboys and bulls had paraded under the lights. In fact, my Mama and Daddy and Aunt Bess are buried in the spot that was once just about dead center of the rodeo ring.

I still have trouble realizing how quickly time and trees come to reclaim and grow over what once was there. When I go home now, I still expect to see things the way they were. But everything has changed – and a lot of what used to be is gone forever. Pastures that were open and clear are filled with Jim Walters homes; the wonderful clear creek that ran through Horace Cato's pasture is little more than a dirty ditch filled with garbage and tires and grown over with briers and vines, and the Humble Oil Company Camp where my best friend Ann Alworth lived has now mostly been reclaimed by pine trees.

Between those times when rodeos and movie cowboys and circuses and calliopes and big dead whales were imported for excitement, I found pleasure and excitement in the natural world. Sometimes in small, simple displays, like the sight of dozens of flickering lightning bugs rising from the grass for the first time each summer, and other times like the awesome cosmic light show of the Leonid meteor shower in the fall. While seeing the first flicker of a lightning bug in the summer always made me inexplicably happy, catching the swift flash of a shooting star streaking across the sky made me gasp, literally drop my jaw and whisper "aaahhhh!"

The first time I saw the Leonid shower, Mama and Daddy and my friend Jackie Bailey and I were riding back home from the Mississippi State Fair in Jackson. The Fair itself was always good for a big pop of adrenaline. Stepping onto the Midway was tantamount to stepping into Alice's Wonderland. The sensory assault was overwhelming – all glowing, whirling color mixed with the unmistakable sounds of rides and barkers and carousel music and the smells of all the treats a child dreams of – popcorn, peanuts, candied apples on a stick, and best of all – cotton candy.

I was always too scared to ride the Ferris wheel or anything that went airborne, but I rode everything that stayed on the ground, no matter how fast it went, and I rode the merry-go-round long after I was too old and just looked silly on the little horses, but I loved the music it played. I lost way too many dimes throwing

balls at stuffed monkeys and stacked bottles and putting them
down on colored circles while a man spun an arrow around a big
wheel of nails.

Daddy, who usually refused to go anywhere, got a little aberrant and was just plain fun to be with at the fair where his inner
little boy came out to play. I can still see him pushing back his
hat and putting his elbow down on the counter and taking aim
with a gun that shot corks at rows of moving ducks trying to win
a cheap little bear for me.

When we left the fairgrounds and headed back to the car that
night, I thought surely nothing on earth could top the Mississippi
State Fair for sheer raw excitement. And I was right – nothing *on
earth* could.

On the way home, Jackie and I sat in the back seat and jabbered
for a while about all we had just seen and done and snickered and
giggled the way little girls do for no apparent reason. Then we
settled into quietness. Jackie went to sleep, and I sat still. I was just
riding through the darkness staring out the back window when
all of a sudden at the exact same moment, not one, not two, but
three shooting stars streaked across the sky – and then another
and soon another. I screamed for Mama to look. Jackie waked up
and Daddy slowed down so he could look too, and for the rest of
the drive home as the earth passed through a dying comet's tail,
we watched as a lifetime supply of burning embers ignited and
flamed and died before our eyes.

The next day Mama tried to answer all my questions and
explain to me what caused the spectacular light show, but I still
had questions, so I did what I always did when Mama and Daddy
couldn't satisfy my curiosity. I looked it up in my *World Book
Encyclopedia*. Turned out that what I had seen had a name – *Leonid*
– and that seeing it didn't have to be a once-in-a-lifetime experience because the earth would pass through the debris of the
comet's tail again and again in other Falls. I found it comforting to
know, not only that I might see that light show again, but also that

the movement of all those suns and moons and stars and planets was not a wholly random phenomenon. There was, I discovered, a predictable regularity to cosmic motion.

A few years later, in another Fall, I read or heard that the earth would soon pass through that comet's tail again. The night of its coming, I asked Daddy to park our car between our garage apartment and Lyda and Stinky's and I took a blanket and pillow out and lay down on top of the car and waited. Because buildings and pecan trees framed a slice of the sky for me, I had a much smaller window on the universe than the one we had riding home from the fair, but I was lucky that night. The tilt of the earth and the path of the comet's tail converged nicely right over Brookhaven, and once again I was dazzled by dozens of streaking stars.

It's a lot harder now to see shooting stars. Sometimes on the night of the Leonid shower, clouds obscure them, and living in a city, artificial lights always make it a lot harder to see the stars in the sky.

Just a few years ago, the night Leonid was to pass, I got the old urge again and late the night of the shooting stars shower got in the car and drove out from Atlanta hoping to get a clear view so I could see one more light show. I never did get far enough away from the light clutter of town, but my daughter, Amy, who then lived on a farm away from bright lights got up at 4:00 in the morning and went out to look for the shooting stars.

The next day she told me that when she first went outside the sky was cloudy, but somehow, almost miraculously at just the right time winds blew the clouds away, the sky cleared and she and her husband, Will Goodnight, saw a few shooting stars.

And you know what, I bet that one day my grandchildren, Nellie and Crawford and Jamie and Wyatt and Emmaline, will go out on a cool crisp Fall night to watch as the earth passes through that same comet's tail.

I find that very comforting.

Danger Zones: DDT, Stick Shifts and Fire

I didn't think about danger too much when I was growing up in Brookhaven, Mississippi, in the 40s and 50s. After all, it wasn't called "The Homeseekers Paradise" for nothing. I never knew anyone there who was the victim of a violent crime. The *Brookhaven Leader Times* was filled more with reports of social events, weddings, births and obituaries than with accounts of mayhem and murder.

Mama and Daddy, as one would expect from parents who had been married for twelve years before their only child was born, were forever warning me about danger and reminding me to be careful, but back then they were warning me about things like keeping both hands on the handle bars while riding my bike backwards, looking both ways before crossing a street, or climbing no higher than my head up the fig trees in back of Uncle Frank's warehouse or the monkey bars on the playground.

After I turned fourteen and they started letting me drive the car without a license, when they said "be careful," what they really meant was "don't drive too fast," a warning that usually went unheeded as soon as I turned the corner and was out of sight. They weren't worried about me getting a ticket because all of the

172

policemen in town knew most of the teenagers in town by name, and they were also pretty much satisfied to let parents decide when their kids were old enough to drive. For some parents, the main criterion for being driving-ready was getting tall enough to see over the steering wheel and reach the pedals at the same time.

Once you met that requirement, either your Mama or your Daddy, whichever one had the stronger nerves and the most patience, took you out to the Brookhaven Airfield, showed you how to shift gears on the old floorboard stick shift, pointed to the gas pedal, told you to push the clutch in and then said, "Okay, now take your foot off it – slowly."

Since there was no airport building at what we called the airport, and no one that I knew of had a private plane to keep there, it was pretty much an airport in name only. It was just a long open swath of grass that someone kept mowed so planes could land and take off from there. Because there were no fences or structures anywhere in sight, the learning driver could buck and grind gears and twist and turn the steering wheel with reckless abandon without coming close to hitting anything.

For years Daddy had from time to time let me sit between his legs and steer the car while he worked the pedals and gave instructions. Mama couldn't bear to. In spite of the fact that she was the outgoing, gregarious, funny one, she also was the seriously nervous one, so Daddy was my Driver's Ed teacher.

On our first lesson I had our car bucking around like one of the Brahma bulls at the traveling rodeo show, but Daddy kept calm and just kept saying over and over:

"Slow, now slow – and smooth. I said take your foot off the clutch slow and smooth."

In spite of my tendency to drive that old beige Dodge as fast it would go, I don't think I was ever a real danger to myself or anyone else. The car didn't fare quite so well. Backing out of the garage one time, I took off most of the right front fender coming out on a diagonal instead of straight, and I blew a hole in the muffler doing my favorite car trick. When I passed one of my friends house, I'd turn off the ignition, let some gas build up and then switch the ignition back on to make the car backfire. One time I left the ignition off too long, too much gas built up, and the re-ignition blew a huge hole in the muffler. I hated it when Daddy got the car fixed because I loved the sound of the rumble and roar of the un-muffled engine and I never told him how I busted the hole in it.

Later, when we moved out in the country Mama and Daddy's warnings about danger meant things like "watch out for snakes" or "don't drown yourself" which they believed were real possibilities because of my habit of wading up to my armpits in creeks and lakes and ponds, pushing through lily pads and logs to get to the best fishing spots because even then I knew intuitively that fish knew instinctively that the best place to be a fish was in the place it was the very hardest for humans to reach. I waded into some really snaky places.

Their fears for my safety were pretty much unfounded. My whole life has been about as far removed from real danger as a life is apt to be. I've never witnessed death, a violent act, or even a really bad car accident. And the only fight I ever saw was the day the pudgy Goss twins jumped on L. M. Gartman at school and began pummeling him because he teased them about being fat until they couldn't take it any more.

In retrospect, I've decided that probably the single most dangerous thing I did as a child was play war in the street with a bunch of kids following the municipal mosquito-killing machine as it drove up one street and down another, spewing out a smoke screen of toxic DDT vapors. Bird and Ronny and I pretended it was battlefield smoke and followed right behind the machine in the middle of the street, lobbing pine and magnolia cones pretending they were hand grenades. Ronny's cousin Kackie, our other sometime playmate, usually sat out when we played this game. We thought it was because she was too sissy to play war, but she said her mother wouldn't let her because it made her cough and wheeze.

Though I lived my childhood outside of real physical danger zones, my Daddy, the fireman, didn't. Once, he was cutting through a door with an axe when it slipped and cut clean through his boot and deep into his foot. Another time, he was burned badly on his neck by molten dripping roof tar. And he almost got killed when James Williams, a teenaged pyromaniac, tried to burn the town to the ground.

The first fire James set didn't arouse too much suspicion. One Sunday night, a fire broke out downtown up in the second floor of a building on Main Street that had an unlocked stairwell leading from the sidewalk up into a long wooden hall with lawyers' and accountants' offices and a beauty shop flanking its sides. Not a whole lot of damage was done. Someone running late for Sunday night service at the First Methodist Church spotted the fire pretty quickly. The regular firemen got there fast and put it out, and Daddy who was no longer a live-in, full-time fireman, just a member of the volunteer brigade, didn't even get called in.

The next Sunday night at about the same time, a fire broke out in an open stairwell that led up into second floor offices over the bank and the Buster Brown shoe store next door. This time, somebody on the way to Sunday night service at the First Baptist Church passed by, smelled smoke, called the fire station and real disaster was again averted.

Mama and her best friend, Irma Foster, whose business, the Brookhaven Specialty Shop, was only two doors down from the second fire, and pretty much everybody else in Brookhaven started talking about what a coincidence it was, having two fires start inside the second floor hallway of two buildings with open stairwells at pretty much the same time on two consecutive Sunday nights. The more analytical thinkers in town, in fact, anyone who knew something about probability and co-variability, were certain that the fires were intentionally set.

Since I had lived at the fire station and played with the firemen and all the old men who sat around the fire station playing checkers and dominoes and gin rummy, I knew more than the average child about causes of fire and I personally thought it might be a couple of cases of spontaneous combustion, mainly because that was the only explanation I'd ever heard of to *explain* fires of *unexplained* origin.

One summer when crops were being fried in the fields and our old oscillating fan did nothing but whine and whirl hot air around the room, Ben Munn, Uncle Bud's closest neighbor's barn caught fire and burned to the ground. When Uncle Bud told us about the fire, he said it was caused by spontaneous combustion. No lightning strikes. No wiring problems. No wiring – period. In fact, some of Uncle Bud's neighbors were still using kerosene lamps in their houses back then. No sinister suspicious strangers within ten miles. Nobody with any reason to burn Ben Munn's barn down. Just spontaneous combustion. First time I ever heard of such a thing.

Daddy, the fireman, explained it to me. He said that the old tin roof on the barn got so hot and made the dry hay under it so hot that it just burst into flames. Like the burning bushes in the Bible. The problem, of course, with my theory was that the Brookhaven fires were being started in the evening in early Spring in dark cool halls that were devoid of hay or other spontaneous combustibles.

You could almost feel the collective holding of breath as the third Sunday night came and went without another fire alarm. On Monday there was a palpable and collective sigh of relief, but relief that only lasted a week.

I don't remember for sure where I was on either of the first two Sunday fires, but as I recall, the next Sunday after the break in the fires was Easter Sunday, and I went to Sunday School and church in the morning and back again for evening service that night. By myself. Mama, who had faithfully toted me to Sunday School every Sunday when I was little, pretty much stopped going with me after I got a little older and took Jesus for my own personal Savior. Figuring that she had done her duty hauling me off to Sunday School and church until it "took" and I had, as I would say now, internalized my commitment to Christ, I was pretty much on my own with God.

So I was sitting up in the back row of the right side balcony, still wearing the Easter suit Mama had made me that year. It was a hot pink linen skirt, a white blouse with a lacy collar, and a matching hot pink bolero style jacket. She'd also made me wear an old-lady-looking felt hat with fake flowers to church that morning, but decided that unlike little Catholic girls who were supposed to keep their heads covered every time they entered the sanctuary, little Baptist girls didn't have to wear hats to church at night.

Brother Miller was just getting warmed up on his favorite sermon topic, "One's Christian Duty to Tithe" when the lights went out in the sanctuary. Even though the power was obviously off, the sanctuary was glowing with an unreal, orange light flickering through the stained glass window. Light from a huge fire. To this day, I have no idea if anyone else, or if everyone else got up and left the church, but I did, and as soon as I was outside, I could see that half a block of Main Street, a block and a half away from the church was in flames.

It was the biggest fire I had ever seen. As it turned out, it was the biggest fire Brookhaven had ever had or, as far as I know, has had since then.

I started running toward the fire. When I crossed the railroad tracks and got to the edge of the block that was on fire, everything was chaos. Just about everyone in town had been drawn to the fire and was standing in the street – hypnotized and horrified. Both dime stores were being consumed by flames and for a second or two I was worried about where I would spend my allowance with both Morgan and Lindsey and Woolworth's going up in flames. All the stores from Woolworth's to Grafton's Drug Store on the corner across from the Post Office were in flames. Everything. Samuel's Appliance Shop, a beauty parlor, Grafton's Drug Store and everything on the second floor above them.

There was a firewall on top of the buildings dividing the roofs where flames had not yet broken through the roof from the ones where it had. When I looked up, I saw my Daddy standing on top of that wall holding a hose and shooting water into the East side of Woolworth's and everything on the second floors above them. I was still looking up and watching Daddy when the West side wall of Grafton's collapsed and the falling bricks ruptured a gas line that ran from the store to the street. Then new flames from that rupture started shooting into the air through the hole the falling bricks had gouged in the sidewalk.

I started to run toward the flames and my Daddy, but something or someone stopped me. I heard somebody say, "Honey, you can't go any closer" so I started walking backwards like a crawfish because I couldn't take my eyes off the real life inferno. It was far more spectacular than any movie fire I'd ever seen. I should have turned around and looked where I was going, but instead I took a couple of steps backward and tripped and fell over one of the big pressure hoses filled with water that was writhing around in the street.

Someone helped me up. I wasn't hurt, but when I looked down at my new Easter suit, it was now stained with sooty run-off water and ripped across the bottom. Right then I knew I had to find my Mama. From the day I was born until the day my parents left me alone on the campus of Mississippi State College for Women, I was a real clingy Mama's baby. I always panicked when I didn't know where Mama was, and now, with Daddy on top of a burning building and my homemade Easter dress ruined,

I knew I had to find her. She had to hold me and hug me and tell me everything was okay.

We only lived a block away from where the fire was devouring the dime stores, so I started running down the street past Janie's Bakery, the Dixie Theatre, the A&P and City Hall. I hit the bottom of the steps up to the garage apartment screaming for my Mama, terrified as much because I had ruined my Easter suit as because I had just seen my Daddy on top of a burning building. I didn't want my Daddy to get hurt, but I also didn't want Mama to pinch her lips and get all mad at me about the suit when I needed her love and reassurance so badly.

But Mama wasn't there.

So I turned and ran back to the corner of the burning block and started asking everyone I knew if they'd seen my Mama. The fact was that I knew just about everybody I saw that night and everybody knew me because long before anybody heard that "it takes a village" to raise a child, folks in Brookhaven were already doing it that way.

Somebody pointed me toward the corner of the State Bank building. Mama was over there with Miss Mary Myers, the fire chief's wife. You could tell they were both upset and trying not to cry. When I got to Mama, I just went limp and though I was way too big to be held like a baby, she picked me up and hugged me really tight for a long time and then put me down and held my hand.

I never figured out what it was about Mama that was so primally soothing. Sometimes I thought it was because she always smelled so good. Sometimes I thought it was because her voice was so mellow and warm. She didn't talk country like some of her siblings and most all of her cousins. She did prolong her internal vowel sounds a little bit – just enough to make her regular talking sometimes sound like she was singing. She sounded more like folks who lived up in the Mississippi delta – the ones that talked with what we called *magnolia mouths* – than like people in Lincoln

County. All I knew was that when I was sick or scared or fell or was worried or wounded and sad, and if Mama wasn't drinking, all she had to do to make me feel good was hug me and say the magic words "everything's gonna be all right, darlin'." And it would be.

There was something about Mama that made people like her and want to be around her. Her eyes were a warm dark brown. Not the deep dark almost-black-dark-brown of Italian eyes or Spanish eyes. Just a warm dark brown. She went to the beauty parlor once a week, put cold cream on her face every night, plucked her eye-brows to thin lines and then drew them back on with an eyebrow pencil, and always wore make-up, perfume and costume jewelry when she went out. I have no idea if my Mama was ever really happy, but if she wasn't, she sure put on a good front. She smiled a lot and laughed a lot, but mostly – now that I think about it – when other people were around. Like company manners and Sunday clothes that you put on for special occasions and other people, Mama always put on a smile when she was out of the house. And she talked a lot to everybody – people she knew, people she didn't know, customers, her sisters and brothers, the black men who worked at the service station and most of all to me. She talked to me a lot, and as a child, I only felt whole and complete when I was with my Mama and she was smiling. I literally couldn't stand to be away from her. Especially not at night. I was pretty old before I actually managed to spend a whole night at my friend Jackie Bailey's house.

It became some sort of sad charade that we played again and again. Jackie would invite me to spend the night at her house, and I would be excited and Mama would put my pajamas in a grocery sack and drive me over to Jackie's house and she and I would start to play and Mama and Nell Bailey would gossip some and then Mama would kiss me goodbye and drive away, and I'd keep playing for awhile, but I knew as soon as the car was out of sight that I'd be going home before dark.

One time when I was seven or so, I made up my mind that I was going to stop being a Mama's baby and really do it – spend a whole night away from home. After Mama left, Jackie and her cousin, Raymond Foster, who lived next door and I started playing a game we called *parachute*. Raymond who was a couple of years older than Jackie and me and a lot bigger would lie down on the ground and put his feet up in the air, bend his knees, and Jackie and I would take turns sitting on his bare feet. Then he'd thrust his legs upward, and we'd go flying high, and hit the ground rolling and laughing. That evening we kept telling Raymond to push us harder and make us go higher and higher. On my last turn, he launched me higher than ever, but when I hit the ground I wasn't rolling or laughing. I landed with my right arm under my butt and when I did, both bones snapped just above the wrist.

I'll never forget how funny it looked. The bones didn't break the skin, but they went up together under the skin in a big V-shape like a drawbridge when it's raised. It looked like I had two elbows and one of them was in the wrong place. I screamed. Not so much because of the pain, but because I knew arms were never supposed to look like that. Jackie and Raymond screamed too and Nell Bailey came running out of the kitchen and almost fainted. Then she started screaming too, so Jack, Jackie's Daddy came out and started yelling at Nell like it was her fault. Then Raymond's mother, Nell's sister, came out to see what was going on. She was a crippled woman with one leg a lot shorter than the other was so she dipped way over to one side when she walked. She looked at my arm and then she looked at Nell the way big sisters do and very calmly said, "Nell, you need to take this child to the hospital. I'll take care of the kids."

By this time, I'd stopped screaming and just kept saying "I want my Mama." Nell started to take me to the hospital, which we had to pass to get to my house, but I begged her just to take me to my Mama, so Nell drove right past the hospital and took me home. When we got there, Mama was standing outside the house talking to Bird's mom, Celeste Cassals, and when they saw us coming up the driveway, they both started laughing, sure that once again I was playing sick or using some other excuse to get Nell to bring me home.

Mama came over to the car, looked in the window, saw my extra elbow and realized that my pain and my tears were real. She opened the door and got in the car and put her arms around me and held me and said the magic words I had to hear,

"It's okay, darlin'. Everything's gonna be all right." And it worked. She held me close and it really didn't hurt any more. Instead of telling Nell to take me to the hospital, she told her to take me over to Dr. Marquette's house. Dr. Marquette had delivered me, and every pill and shot I'd ever had had been administered by Doc Marquette and he lived on the same street we did, but on past the elementary school where the houses were big and nice.

Nell tore into his driveway honking her horn and jumped out and ran up to his door almost before the car stopped. Mama just kept hugging me. Dr. Marquette came out, looked at my arm and told Nell to follow him to the hospital. In the emergency room, he took my arm and my hand and pulled them in opposite directions and the bones snapped back down where they belonged and he put a cast on my arm and Nell drove us home.

Not long after that I did spend an entire night at Jackie Bailey's house. It was strange. Nell came in before she turned out the lights and reached down and hugged Jackie and came over and hugged me too, to make me feel at home and loved. That was nice of Nell to do that, I thought, and I didn't say anything because I didn't want to be impolite or hurt her feelings, but I knew for sure at that moment that all Mamas' hugs weren't the same, and that only *my* Mama's touch could make pain go away and make me believe that at least for a little while, everything would be all right.

So the night of the big fire when Mama held me and said, "Everything's gonna be all right, darlin'," I believed her. Daddy worked at the fire all night, staying around to help control hot spots and came home sooty and smelling of smoke the next morning, but he was safe.

The morning after the fire, with half of Brookhaven's Main Street lying in smoldering piles of boards and bricks, the notion that the three fires, set in three open second-story hallways on three Sunday nights at about the same time were a coincidence was abandoned. It was clear to everyone that there was an arsonist in town.

Mama tried to talk to Daddy about it. "What do you think, Gordon?"

"About what?"

"Who do you think set the fire? How do you think they did it?

Daddy didn't say a word. He just shrugged his shoulders and walked away.

Mama could usually translate Daddy's monosyllabic responses. She could tell the difference between "uh huh" (yes) and "unh uh (no)." To me his *yes* grunts and his *no* grunts were indistinguishable. But she could get nothing out of Daddy about his thoughts on the fire.

Nothing stopped Mama and Irma and all the ladies at the Brookhaven Specialty Shop from gossiping and speculating up a storm. Irma and Miss Laura Jane Hough were partners in a little boxcar-sized women's clothing store. All Mama's lady friends hung out there like the old men did at the fire station. They sat in the "gossip box" at the back of the store behind the last clothes rack at a little table where the ladies smoked and drank Coca Colas and Irma played solitaire between customers.

One of the regular ladies was Josie Barlow, whose husband,

Mr. Barlow, was the District Attorney and knew everything that went on at the courthouse. Thursday, Josie came in the Specialty Shop and dropped a tidbit to feed the rumor machine.

"Y'all will never guess what Mr. Barlow told me about the fires. Of course, you know – I mean – I really can't tell anyone."

"Can't tell us what, Josie?"

"Well, they think they know who did it."

"They know who started the fires?"

"Well, I know something about..." Josie caught herself and stopped before using a pronoun that would have given a clue about the arsonist's gender, "the person who did it."

"Who? Josie Barlow, you better tell us."

"Well, you know," Josie teased, "you know I want to tell y'all, but Mr. Barlow would kill me if I did."

Over the years, Josie had gleaned all sorts of bits and pieces of information from Mr. Barlow that she shared with her friends in the gossip box, always, of course, exacting a promise that what she told Mama and Irma and Cat Jackson and Miss Hough would never "leave this room." And, of course, they promised and they, of course, meant it when they promised, or at least they meant they would only tell one other person. In reality Mama meant she wouldn't tell anybody but Daddy, and that branch of the rumor tree usually stopped there because he didn't much care about knowing anything Mama talked about with the women at the Specialty Shop, and if he did – Gordon Meese would never tell anybody. But Irma told Vernon, Cat told Dewey and Miss Hough told Miss Craig the lady she and her little Pekingese lived with. Then in a perversion of the old "each one, teach one" doctrine, Dewey told his Daddy, Old Man Jackson, Vernon told Ed James who owned the taxi cab stand where Vernon hung around and answered the phone from time to time – they told only their wives, and so on. So gossip spread exponentially from the gossip box and in less than a week after Josie shared one of her secrets, there was no one left to tell the secret to.

Essentially there were no secrets in Brookhaven. What *one* knew – in a matter of time – everyone would know.

The identity of the arsonist, if she really knew it, was the biggest gossip coup Josie ever got wind of from Mr. Barlow, and she wanted to let it out more than she had ever wanted to do anything, but she also knew Mr. Barlow would just as soon have her arrested as anybody else if she messed up this one, so as bad as she wanted to take center stage and play "guess who done it?" with the girls, she made a motion as if zipping her lips, crossed her arms, reared back in her chair, sucked her unfiltered Lucky Strike and said no more. The gossip box was closed, but word was soon out on all the grapevines in town *"they have a suspect."* Josie never got to tell who the suspect was. Whoever the authorities thought it was, they were wrong.

As it turned out, it wasn't the police chief or sheriff or district attorney who broke the case. Law enforcement officials in town had followed the most obvious trail, going around to all the service stations in town asking if any suspicious strangers had come around buying kerosene. They were only looking for strangers because they were positive that no one who lived in Brookhaven would deliberately try to burn the town down.

Apparently, when a reporter from Jackson came to town to do a story about the Brookhaven fires, he skipped the service stations and went right straight to all the drug stores in town. Not counting Grafton's which was one of the stores destroyed in the Main Street fire there were four other drug stores in town. When the reporter asked one of the druggists if he'd been selling more lighter fluid than usual lately, he nodded as it dawned on him that his best cigarette lighter fluid customer for the past few weeks had been a gawky, acned, teen-aged boy.

Though Daddy didn't usually waste time on idle speculation, he was pretty quick to judge the facts once they were in. He didn't blame the fire on James, though the law did. And he didn't blame his parents for raising a sorry son as Mama and Irma did. He blamed the drug store.

"What did that stupid son of a bitch think a thirteen-year old boy was doing with a bucket of lighter fluid?"

Apparently, James bought lighter fluid every Saturday morning before each of the fires. His MO was pretty simple. On his way to church, he went up the stairs into a hallway, doused some tissue with lighter fluid and struck a match. The old interiors with their heart of pine floors made perfect tinder. Then he walked back out and went on to the First Methodist Church and waited for the fire alarm. The "Big Fire" was right across the street from the Post Office. And the Methodist church was right behind the post office.

After the kid was caught, a Methodist friend of mine remembered he was the first to run out of he church the night of the first fire and that the night of the last big fire he sat on the post office steps, still wearing his choir robe, and watched the flames until the West side wall of Grafton's Drug Store fell and knocked a hole in the sidewalk and ruptured the gas line.

She said he was the last person from the choir to move back and away from the heat and flames.

Slim

 I still believe every little girl who wants a horse ought to have one – even if she lives in a garage apartment across the street from City Hall and sleeps in the dining room on a fold-up rollaway bed.

After years of pure longing and begging for a horse, I finally had one of those "aha" moments that can change your life forever. I realized I was begging for the wrong thing. I was begging for a *horse* when I should have been begging for a *house*. In the country. With some land. And a fence.

This, as it turned out, presented an even bigger problem – one that was deeply rooted in the insecure place in my Daddy's psyche. You see, Daddy and his brothers, Joe and Wayne, didn't take risks. Beneath their skin-thin macho veneer, they were insecure men – so afraid of losing the little they had, they ventured nothing that didn't come with a money back guarantee. Daddy always rented our houses because he was so afraid he couldn't keep up the payments he couldn't bring himself to buy one, and the notion of investing was an even more foreign concept to him. Theoretically, Daddy was willing to buy a house, but not, he said, until he saved enough money to buy one outright. Since he and Mama never managed to save a penny, owning a house on Daddy's terms seemed to be out of the question.

The Meese boys' fears probably stemmed from watching their own Daddy, Joseph Lafayette Meese take bigger and bigger risks with his money and their lives, always upping the ante until he finally bet everything he had on something he couldn't sell – and lost everything.

When Joe Meese left Danville, Illinois, he moved his children, Toots, Blanche, Wayne, Joe, my Daddy, Gordon Eli, and his second wife, Glendora Judd to Tennessee. He bought a bunch of land just outside of what is now downtown Memphis. Then he bought or built (family history is vague on this point) a cotton gin, a general merchandise store and a coffin factory. Though the post office address was Route 1, Lucy, Tennessee, people called the little town Meesetown, and it thrived and he prospered.

My Daddy, who would send his only child to college by saving all the dimes that came into the cash register of his little country store, and who would die wearing faded denim over-alls, grew up with clean finger nails, the pampered son of the patriarch, not just of his family, but all of Meesetown. Daddy had his very own big black horse that he rode wearing herringbone knickers and a cap cocked to the side of his head, and, in a picture I still have, he looked jaunty and privileged.

They say my Granddaddy, Joe Meese, loved music and played the violin, and my cousin Winky told me that Uncle Joe, while cold stone sober, swore to her that his Daddy owned a Stradivarius violin. Understand I'm not saying that I believe it; I'm just repeating what I've heard. True or not, I find it fascinating that such a myth has become a part of Meese family lore.

By all accounts, Granddaddy Meese prospered in Tennessee. Then, in 1924, he decided there was more money to be made in cotton farming and bought a 2800-acre plantation in Copiah County, Mississippi. The columns at the end of the driveway of that plantation are still standing, bearing its name chiseled in marble – *Dixie Gardens*. Dixie Gardens. My Yankee Grandaddy couldn't have picked a more Southern place name. Now that driveway leads to nowhere but an open field.

The Hazlehurst paper carried an article about the arrival of the Meeses from Tennessee and a picture of the two story main house with columns that would have made even Scarlet O'Hara proud.

While Joe was by most accounts a canny businessman, he apparently wasn't smart enough to bet the "don't come line" in the cotton speculation market. He rounded up enough farm hands to get cotton seed in the ground and tease it into bloom and nurse it to maturity. He got it picked and ginned and baled and hauled to Natchez where it sat on the docks by the river while he waited for the price per bale to go up. As he waited, the price fell – and as he waited longer, the price fell more. But Joe Meese was a stubborn man so he kept on holding his cotton until the market completely crashed and his cotton was essentially worthless. He was completely wiped out and Dixie Gardens was sold. Not long after that he died, a drinking, angry, grieving man and Glendora Judd Meese, the proud Quaker woman from Vermillion Grove, Illinois, wound up working in Raymond, Mississippi, as a kind of housemother in a group home for the mentally impaired.

And my Daddy, stunned by the death of his invincible father and the loss of his own privileged place in the world, quit school and went to work. For most of the rest of his life he earned his living working for other men – at a service station, a tire recapping place when rubber and tires were precious during the war, and as a fireman. And he always rented the roof he put over his wife and daughter's head. "Nothing ventured; nothing gained" for Gordon Meese meant "Nothing risked – nothing lost." If owning a business was risky, owing a mortgage for thirty years was beyond risky, so for most of his life, Daddy owned nothing. Unless you count old used cars.

His brothers fared no better. So you see, the Meese men's

ingrained insecurities stood as the major obstacle between me and my horse.

Mama, on the other hand, was a natural ally. She wanted a house of her own every bit as much as I wanted a horse. For years she read the house ads in the Brookhaven paper and once she actually got Daddy to ride past a house out on North Jackson Street.

Finally, when I was fifteen, a real harmonious convergence occurred. The Lamberts out on Enterprise Road told Cat Jackson's sister, Thelma Case, that they were going to sell their house and she told Cat and Cat told Mama who mentioned it to Daddy. Mama and I wanted to drive out and take a look that very day, but Daddy resisted for a day or two. Then after he closed the station one day, instead of turning the car toward home, he headed out Enterprise Road.

This time Daddy, not only rode past the house, he turned around and went back and forth past it a time or two and then stopped the car and got out and started talking to Mr. Lambert who was sitting barefoot on his front porch. I can't imagine they had much of a conversation because Mr. Lambert was cut from the same conversational cloth as Daddy. Daddy wouldn't go inside the house, but he walked all around it and then he and Mr. Lambert went down toward the trees at the back of the pasture, pointing to unseen lines that marked the property boundaries.

Miz Lambert and a bunch of dirty little Lamberts and Mama and I stood out in the front yard for a while talking about potted plants. Mama loved flowers and I knew she was hinting for Miz Lambert to offer her a cutting of her hen and biddies plant. When I looked down at the ground, I realized there wasn't a blade of grass to be seen in front of the house because the Lamberts scraped the yard bare and swept it with broom sage to keep from having to mow grass. I was standing in a dust bowl where with every step wisps of gray powder puffed up and coated my shoes.

It was clear that Miz Lambert didn't want to invite Mama

in to look around the house and equally clear that Mama was dying to get inside. They hemmed and hawed until finally Miz Lambert blinked. She tried to ask Mama in, as southern hospitality demanded, but in a way that would discourage acceptance. "Well, Miz Meese, I'd like to ask you to come in, but I'd hate for anybody to see my house like it is *today* (she emphasized *today* suggesting that while her house was *today* a mess and a half, she was normally a clean and tidy person). I did my wash this morning, and I ain't made the beds yet and I ain't washed the dishes and...."

Mama interrupted her with an assurance that it didn't matter; she wouldn't notice and her house was a mess too.

I could tell Mama was really getting her hopes up. The Lambert place was totally lacking in what real estate agents today call "street appeal." It wasn't much more than a box covered with asbestos siding. A covered porch ran across the front and there were two flimsy screened doors on it and two windows. But it had a roof and a floor of sorts, and so met Mama's definition of a home. Nothing, however, prepared Mama for Miz Lambert's mess. She might have washed that morning, but mounds of dirty clothes were still piled everywhere. There were six rooms in all, but no living room, dining room or bedroom as such. There were just rooms pretty much full of beds and dirty clothes and a kitchen. The walls were unpainted. The floors were unpainted pine boards with cracks between them so wide you could see their chickens scratching under the house. There was no indoor bathroom.

Well, Mama just got sick and quiet and wavered. At that moment, I think she lost the will to buy a house and was ready to go back to the garage apartment and give up. Personally, I wasn't much interested in what it looked like, but it smelled awful in there. I held my breath for a long as I could and ran back outside.

Then a miracle happened. Just when Mama was ready to

throw in the towel, Daddy announced in the car on the way back to town,

"Well, I liked it."

I almost fainted. Mama didn't know what to say. She knew better than to complain about the house after Daddy's first positive sign ever that he might be ready to take a risk, so we rode the rest of the way back to town without saying another word.

For the next few days, Mama and Daddy totally avoided the subject of the house. During that time, Mama apparently decided that a house with cracks in the floor, scraped yard and no indoor bathroom was better than no house at all. But she played it smart. Having seen that one sign of weakness in the chink of Daddy's anti-house-buying-armor, she waited. She knew that a frontal assault would meet resistance and arguments would just raise counter arguments. I don't think I'd ever seen her show so much restraint. She just kept waiting for Daddy to make the next move. And finally he did. With two startling pronouncements: (1) "I was thinking we might build a little store out there and put in a grease rack, and (2) you reckon Frank Hartman would lend us some money? I ain't going to no damn bank." Daddy said the latter in a way that suggested he rejected banks, but that was just his way of covering up his fear that the bank would reject him.

Daddy having said that, Mama knew that the next move was hers. She knew there was no way in hell Gordon Meese would himself get up the nerve to ask Frank Hartman or anybody else to lend him money, but in "Daddyspeak," he had also just tacitly announced that he wanted Mama to do it.

The details were never clear to me how it happened, but it did happen. Mama asked her second cousin's husband for a loan, and he said *yes* and every month after we moved to the country, Leander drove Uncle Frank over to the store and Mama went out and handed Uncle Frank some money. He promised Mama that when he died, the place would be hers free and clear, but the executor of his estate apparently never got that message.

So Gordon Meese bought a house. In the country. With land. And a fence. Of course, his country place was only 2791 acres smaller than Dixie Gardens, but finally Daddy owned something.

His brother, Joe, a skilled finish carpenter, came down and built a little box of a store out on the corner of the property and the Brookhaven Pure Oil Co. put in a hydraulic grease rack powerful enough to lift Warren Holmes' big milk hauling trucks and Virgil Wright's big cattle-hauling trucks off the ground and grease them. No other country store in Lincoln County – probably no other country store in the state of Mississippi had a grease rack as good as Daddy's.

Then Uncle Joe went to work on the house. He hung sheet-rock, divided the backroom into a closet and a bathroom, laid some streaky green Armstrong linoleum on the kitchen floor and put down beautiful shiny blond hardwood floors in all the other rooms.

Finally, Daddy had his super grease rack and was his own boss. Mama had hardwood floors to die for. Daddy planted a dozen catalpa trees out back and went over to W. K. White's house to pick some worms off his trees for starters. Mama put potted plants in every container she could find and made the front porch a veritable obstacle course of spider plants, Christmas cacti, and long spiky mother's-in-law tongues.

Mama and Daddy were set for country living. But I still didn't have a horse.

When the Lamberts moved, they left us a bunch of scrawny frustrated hens, but no rooster. I had begged Daddy to get them to leave their goat and they agreed, so my first country pets were the Lambert's leftovers.

The goat, a Billy, named Billy, was very affectionate, and very aggressive. He bonded with me immediately and I found out real fast that having a nuzzly goat for a pet is not a lot of fun. In the first place, Billy smelled awful. And after a few minutes with him, so did I. I tried giving him a bath, using at Mama's suggestion baking soda or Murphy's Oil Soap. I used them both, but all that got me was a sudsy still stinking goat with baking soda caked in his hair.

The other problem with Billy was he followed me everywhere, including into the house. Every time I left him outside and went in the house, he kept butting the back door. He also would rear up on his back legs and try to put his front ones on my shoulders. The first time he did this, I thought it was cute, but it got old soon because he was a big, heavy goat, and now that I think back on it I suspect the raring up on me was some kind of goat sex thing – like a humping dog.

Mama got tired real quick of sweeping goat poop balls off the porch and told me I had to keep Billy tied out behind the tilting, tin-roofed out-building the Lambert boys had built with a conspicuous lack of carpentry skill. So I got a big thick rope and led Billy out to exile, tied him to a fence post and went back in the house. Almost before I could get an orange crush out of the icebox, I heard the familiar butting and banging on the door. There stood Billy with a piece of the rope in his mouth.

I gave up. Mama called Miz Lambert and asked if they would like to have Billy back. We were surprised that they didn't make us pay them to take him off our hands like in the "Ransom of Red Chief," but the next morning, Daddy borrowed Sam Robin's cattle truck and my boyfriend, Sonny Passmore (who was, by the way, Uncle Frank's second wife's adopted son) and I got Billy and took him over to the Lambert's new old house. They'd already "Lambertized" it. Most of the stuff they'd moved was still in bags and boxes and piles on the front porch. When we drove up, Mr. Lambert was sitting on the front steps while his older boys scraped off all the grass around the house. This was not uncommon out in the country where folks either didn't own a lawnmower, were too lazy to use one, or just had a natural preference for gray powdered or red clay lawns over green grassy ones.

With the goat gone and the chickens disinclined to bond with humans, I went into the next phase of my get-a-horse plan. By now I was in the eleventh grade and sensed that my horse getting time was running out.

Daddy had a friend named J.P. Leggett who had claimed for years that he owned a fine Tennessee Walking horse and a trick horse to boot that was running loose in a pasture near Bogue Chito. Since his only child, Peggy, was only three, he told Daddy that I could *have* the horse for as long as I wanted him or until his Peggy was old enough to ride. Problem was, J.P. couldn't catch him, and in fact, wasn't sure he was still alive because he hadn't even seen him in a couple of months.

I set out hounding J.P. to keep trying to catch the horse he said was named "Slim."

"Have you seen him yet? Can you catch him? When are you going to try again?"

"No. Yes. Soon," he would say, always putting me off. This went on for a few months. I was just about to give up, suspecting that maybe J.P. was lying, that maybe he didn't even own a horse, when out of the blue, I met Slim.

I was playing tennis with Soren Daniels over at the old broken down courts at Whitworth College when J.P. drove up, got out, walked up to the court, looked at me, and said,

"You want a horse?"

I whooped and hollered, threw my racquet over to Soren and took off with J.P. headed for Bogue Chito. When we got there, we drove past a burned-out trailer, turned on to some muddy ruts at the back of a barn and – BAM! There he was! Slim. The horse of my dreams. Even cooped up in an itty-bitty shabby calf-holding pen, with a tangled, matted mane, he held his head higher than any horse I'd ever seen. He was elegant. And proud. It was in his eyes and the slant of his ears. Everything about him said, "I'm one smart horse."

The minute I looked him in the eye, I fell in love. And I believe he did too. He was my horse now. I knew it and so did he.

But there was still one little problem. I was wearing a pair of tennis shorts. Slim was in Bogue Chito and I lived almost ten miles away.

I looked around and there was no horse-hauling trailer in sight, so I asked J.P., "How am I supposed to get him home?"

"Ride him."

I must have looked at him as if he were completely insane.

"Or," he added, "if you don't want to, I can let him go again."

"I'll ride him," I said.

J.P. already had a bridle on him. He went over and opened up his car trunk and pulled out an old scarred saddle of brick hard leather with spider webs and bits of mud pods from dirt dauber nests still clinging to it.

When J.P. headed toward him with the saddle, Slim flared his nostrils, laid back his ears and started side-stepping. Every time J.P. took a step toward him, he took another step to the side. I could tell J.P. wanted to muscle him into submission, but I knew that wouldn't work, so I persuaded him to put down the saddle and back off and let me do it. He handed me the bridle and I gave it some slack so there was no pull on Slim and then I walked up to him head on and touched the velvet part of his nose. And I talked to him. I don't have any idea what I said to that horse, but I know it flowed from a lifetime of pent up love from a child waiting for a horse to give it to. And he sensed it.

I could tell J.P. was getting impatient, but I kept patting and nuzzling and whispering to Slim as I led him slowly over to the saddle, picked it up and slid it on to his back, expecting an explosion of horse snorting and rearing (we pronounced it rarin') and kicking. But he just stood there, as if the saddle on his back reminded him of someone else he had loved who had kissed his nose and scratched his ears and climbed up on his back.

He offered no resistance.

I pulled the cinch tight.

No resistance.

I put my foot in the stirrup and pulled on the saddle horn to get up. His name fit him. He was a very tall horse. Slim and tall.

Still no resistance.

Now I wasn't afraid any more, but I could tell that J.P. was getting nervous. It had dawned on him perhaps that if he took Gordon Meese's only daughter to Bogue Chito and got her killed on a wild horse, Gordon Meese would probably kill him.

I can't explain it, but from the first minute I sat astride him, Slim and I understood and loved and trusted each other perfectly. I rode that horse that day ten miles down back country roads. He responded to the barest hint of a touch of the reins to move to the right or the left, to speed up or slow down. He was alert to every sound and all motion – a lizard rustling across a pile of dry leaves or a sweet-gum ball falling to the ground.

I did have one problem though. When J.P. picked me up at the tennis court, I should have gone home and changed clothes. After the first couple of miles, I was beginning to sweat and my bare legs were rubbing on the old rough saddle. Even with Slim's smooth walking horse, rocking horse gait the constant motion was chafing the skin and stretching the tendons in my groin. By the time I got off Slim, all the skin on my inner thighs had been rubbed raw and my muscles were screaming.

J.P. got back to the store long before I did, so Mama and Daddy knew I was on my way. They were sitting on the blue bench waiting for me, nervously puffing on cigarettes, Mama talking too much and too fast the way she did when she was nervous, and Daddy saying absolutely nothing, the way he did when he was nervous.

When I got home I got off and hugged Slim again. His neck was slick and wet with sweat and he smelled just like a horse was supposed to smell. And I loved his smell and was as proud of my new horse as if he had just won the Derby.

As far as I'm concerned nothing is scarier than when you let a new pet go outside alone for the first time. I used to fret with each new puppy or kitten I got. I'd bring them in and smother them with love and gorge them on treats to buy their love and attachment and to assure that when I let them go they would stay – because they wanted to. Daddy's new-pet rule was simple and absolute. All cats and dogs were outdoor pets and couldn't stay inside for loving but for one night. Then it was, "Out it goes!"

One time I got a little mongrel puppy that I called Poppy. I got her when she was only 6 weeks old. I put her in a little box with a blanket and gave her warm milk and smushed up some Vienna sausage for her and held her and hugged her and talked to her and took her outside to pee. I put her box by my bed the first night and when she whimpered I picked her up and put her in my bed and snuggled with her. I played with her all day the next day and begged Daddy to waive the one-day rule, but he wouldn't give in. When I put her box out on the back porch the next night she started whimpering and whining so pitifully that I couldn't stand it. I was afraid she would run off in the night and I'd never see her again. I tried one more time to talk Daddy into letting me bring her back inside, but he told me that if you've got a dog that runs away and doesn't want to stay with you, "you've got a dog that ain't worth having." The next morning when I opened my eyes I popped out of bed and ran to the back porch and looked in Poppy's box and she was lying there curled up in a little furry ball and when she saw me she waggled her little behind and I picked her up and she licked my face.

Still I was worried about letting Slim loose in eight acres of pasture, afraid that if I let him go I would never be able to catch him again. The first night I had him, I closed him up in the little lean-to out back, but clearly he could not spend his life in a stall.

The first morning was a real challenge. In fact, just getting out of bed and walking to the kitchen was a real challenge that day.

Every muscle from my butt to my ankles ached. Walking was a pain; sitting down was utter agony.

But I knew I had to get on Slim again. When I walked out to the shed, I took the bridle with me and I started talking to Slim before he could even see me. When I came around the corner, he turned his beautiful blazed face toward me with ears pricked up. No fear in his eyes. Slim had yielded completely. He trusted me. And as it turned out, he never again trusted anyone but me.

I patted him some and rode him again and then turned him loose. He stood there for a minute. He knew he was free. He looked toward the open pasture and then back at me and began walking along the inside of the fence line, following me like a puppy as I walked back to the store. After that, I knew I could catch him again any time I wanted to. And I could.

Now, as Paul Harvey would say – for the rest of the story. J.P. hadn't lied about Slim being a "trick" horse. He didn't know who taught him or how to get him to "perform" but he knew what tricks he was supposed to know how to do and I figured out how to get him to do them. In fact Slim knew more tricks than any horse I'd ever seen in the movies or on TV. He knew how to pray, getting down on both bent knees, how to take a bow with one knee bent under and the other stretched out, how to sit rump down and forelegs stiff, how to lie down and roll over, how to pose with all four legs placed together in the middle of a very small stump. He knew how to rear up and paw the air on command like a wild stallion.

He also played hide and seek with me. Mama would hold him and I would go hide and then she'd let him go and he'd run all over the yard looking for me behind every tree and the barbecue pit until he found me. Then he would give me a hug. He'd walk right up to me and put his beautiful head over my shoulder and wrap it around behind my neck and nuzzle me.

His *piece de resistance*, however, was playing sick and dead. This involved him lying down and putting his head in my lap. When he did, I'd pat his head and say "poor Slim's so sick" and he would heave his belly, roll his eyes, and make a snorting pitiful sighing sound. Then he would close his eyes and become absolutely still. Playing dead. Fooled a lot of people.

It was a great performance. Bless his heart. As he became more and more famous out on Enterprise Road, everybody who came to the store had to see Jimmie's horse. Sometimes I'd have to catch him three or four times a day to show him off. Even Daddy couldn't conceal how proud he was of his daughter's trick horse. When a new customer or an old friend or relatives from Illinois came to the store, he'd just say,

"Why dont'cha show'em Slim?"

Soon, all it took to catch Slim was to walk out back and whistle. When we weren't performing, my favorite Slim game was to ride him three miles down to the swim hole where Moak's Creek crossed the gravel road. There was a big deep open pool of water there and some boys from Enterprise had hung a rope swing from a big old oak tree limb and somehow attached a strong limber plank to the bank to create a makeshift diving board. That's where Slim and I went swimming together. I'd lead him into the water and hold his mane and he'd swim and pull me around and around in the creek. Even the Enterprise boys who thought they were hotshots shut up and just watched when Slim and I got in the water.

Being a Tennessee Walking horse, his gaits were smooth and when he did the Tennessee walk itself, he arched his neck so proudly that his sheer raw beauty made me cry sometimes then, and as it does now when I think about him. J.P. said he could have been a champion show horse except he strutted with *sooooo* much energy that his back hooves would over-shoot and nick the back of his front hooves. It was like stepping on your own heel.

Slim was absolutely a one-person horse. For as long as I had him, no one else managed to stay on his back. Every single kid who ever saw him wanted to ride him. I'd refuse, telling them,

"I don't mind if you try, but he won't let you."

Willie, a teenaged boy who lived down behind the gravel pit, was so persistent and so sure he could ride Slim that I finally gave in and let him try. I rode Slim right up behind the store near the "domino men" playing at the table under the scrub oaks. Anticipating what was about to happen, they stopped playing and turned to watch. Mama and Daddy and Mr. Dubose came out of the store.

I slid off, handed the reins to Willie and stepped back. Slim turned and assessed the situation. Willie grabbed the saddle horn and pulled himself up on Slim's back. Slim stood still. Willie grinned in triumph for a second, just before Slim went into his wild stallion act. He didn't buck. He never bucked, kicking up his hind legs like a mule. He didn't move his hind legs at all. He just stood straight up and pawed the air and sort of shook himself from side to side. Willie, surprised by the move, fought Slim and gravity briefly, then slid off his back, landing butt first on the ground.

The men turned back to their game. Mama asked him if he'd hurt himself. I asked him perversely if he would like to try again. He said "no" to both questions and after that no one else ever tried to ride him again.

When I started to get up on Slim, he looked back at me with pure mischief in his eyes, almost as if asking, "did you see how I flicked that boy off with no more effort than it takes me to flick flies with my tail?" Then I got on him, and he walked back to the pasture as docilely as an old milk cow.

I never owned Slim. He was just mine on long term loan, so J.P. came and reclaimed him after I went off to college and I never saw him again. He died in a pasture in Bogue Chito. J.P. was never able to catch him again. I think he was waiting for me.

Elvis Presley Junior Smith and Poot

A family of the ubiquitous Lincoln County Smiths moved down the road from our store when I was in the eleventh grade. Red, the Daddy, was just that - red all over. At least all his body parts one could see were red, as were his hair, eyebrows, and whiskers. And when he'd been too much into a bottle of bootleg whiskey, his eyeballs were red too. He was a burly, burly man. Walking muscle. Equal parts redneck and roughneck, Red had a good paying job as foreman on an oil rig in the Malibu oil field east of Brookhaven.

Buddy looked a lot like his daddy, but a softer pudgier Pillsbury Dough Boy version. Every day, sometimes two or three times a day, he'd walk to our store, buy a moon pie and an R.C. Cola (you might think that's an apocryphal version of a typical Southern diet, but it is what Buddy ate), give Mama the exact change, peel that moon pie open, grab it with both hands, pop about a third of it in his mouth at a time, twist his head to one side and then snatch it back again. I don't think I ever saw Buddy actually chew; he just gnawed and gulped like a big ole alligator turtle tearing off chunks of bait. He'd take a bite and then a swig and then a bite and another swig. Other than my fascination with watching Buddy Smith eat moon pies, I remember nothing else about him.

Mama Lola was a local girl, one of umpteen children in the Cline clan. The Cline boys were an odd lot – no two looked anything alike, but the girls were pretty much indistinguishable from each other, except for the way they combed their hair. They all seemed obsessed with seeing how much they could torture, tease, twist and turn their hair, and while they did in most ways look like they'd been cloned, they expressed their individuality in the length, height, color and decorations they chose to adorn their hair. Velma Jane Cline, Lola's sister for whom her daughter, Velma June was named, went for height, pouffing up her thinning ebony tresses until each hair virtually stood on end. Johnny Maye, the sophisticated one, sported a straight red hank that hung to her butt in a swag, which she twitched and tossed the way Slim used his tail to swat flies. She pulled her hair back behind her ears and nailed it down with one of those bands of white artificial roses and babies breath that look so cute on little girls dressed for their first communion and down-right silly on the head of a fiftyish grandmother .

Since red and black and high and hanging hairstyles were already taken by her sisters, Lola went for the curly blonde look. Once when I passed her house, Lola was sitting on her front porch with a towel around her neck and one of her sisters was standing behind her twisting her hair around little plastic curlers to give her a perm. When Mama gave herself a perm, she timed it to the second. Lola and her sisters reasoned that if you left curling stuff on a little while and got a little curl, leaving a perm on for an hour or so would give you lots and lots of curls. The end result was usually a mass, not of curls, but of coarse, wiry stuff, more like yellow Spanish moss than anything you would expect to find on a human's head.

Tipping the scales somewhere on the topside of two hundred, Lola wasn't physically equipped to play the youthful coquette, but that didn't stop her from trying. She and Velma June, who matched her mama pound for pound, wore the same clothes. I don't mean matched outfits. I mean the same clothes. The very same clothes. One day Velma June would come to the store in a black and gold pleated skirt with a satin wrap-around-tie-at-the-waist-blouse and the next day Lola would come in wearing it.

The strangest thing about Velma June and something I've seen since in people whose intelligence quotient hovers around the posted speed limit on an interstate highway, was that when she looked blank, which was most of the time, her blank look could easily be mistaken for deep concentration or superior intelligence.

All-American, the Smith family was not, but for a while they were a family. Red left before daylight in his pick-up truck, Buddy and Velma June stood out front and caught the bus, and Lola came over mid-afternoon and bought stuff to fix supper. I don't think she spent much time on meal planning, and the notion of a food pyramid would have, of course, completely baffled her, but there did seem to be some system driving her purchases. Always when she bought baloney, she bought cheese and onions. Always when she bought sardines or canned salmon, she bought cheese and onions. When she bought red beans, she always bought rice and cheese and onions. She bought lard by the bucketsful. Literally.

It was also pretty clear that Lola knew only two ways to fix food – open cans and pour the contents in a pot and heat it, or if something wasn't in a can and you couldn't pour it in a pot and heat it, coat it with flour and fry it. Even fish. Mama just about fainted one day when she gave Lola some fish we'd caught and found out that she put flour on the fish to fry them. Of all the outrageous things that Lola ever did, I believe the flour on the fish thing shocked Mama the most.

"Darlin'," Mama told me one time "everybody knows that you fry fish with cornmeal." And then as if chanting some Southern cooks mantra, "you put flour on chicken, you put flour on pork chops, and sometimes you even put flour on fatback slab bacon, but you never put flour on fish to fry it."

My Mama never said much about politics, social issues or even religion, but she had oddly strong, even passionate opinions about the most unexpected things, like cornmeal on fish, and pruning azaleas. She was so zealous about not trimming azaleas that she seriously believed it should be against the law in the state of Mississippi to trim azaleas into square shapes like hedges.

Admittedly, there were very few healthy food choices on the shelves of Daddy's store. In fact, the tobacco shelf had more space for Lucky Strikes and Chesterfield and Camels and Garrett's Snuff than the bread rack had room for Sunbeam and Colonial bread.

It didn't matter any way. Near as I can tell Lola never knowingly made healthy nutrition choices. I know for a fact she never bought any milk. She said it was because it would make Buddy and Velma June constipated.

Lola's transformation from a fat, marginally literate homemaker to a certifiable mental case happened pretty quickly. She became a shopaholic. At first, she just started going to town after Red left for work and buying things she didn't need and couldn't use. She bought everything from shoes and nail polish to wax paper and bobby pins. She didn't buy one or two or a package. She bought reams, and boxes, and carloads of things. She bought things that didn't fit, things she couldn't use, things that were already broken. She drove Red Smith nuts.

Red didn't come to the store much because he worked all the time, but once right before he got in his pick-up truck with Buddy and Velma June and left Lola alone in their Jim Walters home for good, Red told Daddy the house was crammed so full of stuff that he had to go out on the back porch just to turn around.

I'm not sure Lola even noticed when Red and her kids left. Her obsessive-compulsive behavior had already begun morphing into another category of mental illness. Once she was alone, she became a full-blown religious fanatic with delusions of saintliness, convinced that she was what she called a "touch healer." She began trying to sidle up and surreptitiously touch the old men who sat in a corner of the store playing dominoes by the gas stove in the winter and out back of the store under the sweet gum trees in the summer when they complained of "arthuritis" or "sick headaches."

Of all the old men who huddled in the corner of the store telling lies and playing dominos, one was very special. Old Man Fonnie Dubose. Most of the men were school dropouts, rednecks, roughnecks, and ne'er-do-wells of one kind or another.

Mr. Dubose was none of the above. He was a real gentleman. He came to the store every day and stayed all day, but he didn't play dominoes. He read newspapers, magazines, and even books. Lola was respectful of Mr. Dubose because he only had one eye and because he was unfailingly courteous to her. She always tried to avoid Daddy.

One day she came in the store and walked right over to Mr. Dubose.

"Feel my hands," she said. "You feel the heat in them, Mr. Fonnie? I got God's power in my hands."

Mr. Dubose looked up from his book and smiled at Lola and asked the most obvious and logical question. "Is that right, Miss Lola, and just how do you know you have God's power in your hands?"

"Because, Mr. Fonnie, I had a puny l'il ole kitten and I thought she was gonna die and I put her on her back and laid my hands on her belly and rubbed it and she started hackin' and retchin' and hauled off and spit out a devil."

"A devil?" Fonnie asked with the natural skepticism of an old man who was still an atheist and had once been an engineer. Casting out kitten devils just did not compute for him.

"Did you see the devil when it came out?" he asked.

"Yes, sir, Mr. Fonnie, I sure did."

"What did it look like?"

"Well, Mr. Fonnie, it was awful looking. It looked like a big ole slimy ball of spit and fur and grass."

At Lola's description of a hairball, Fonnie smiled and looked over at Mama and me, and I think he winked, but he had only one eye and when he shut it, you couldn't tell whether he was winking or blinking.

Lola's claim to have healing power produced one verifiable, though minor miracle. She figured out that it did her no good to be a faith healer if she had nobody to heal, so after the kitty cure thing every time she came over to the store she terrorized the domino men by offering to lay her hands on them wherever they hurt. The net effect of her offer was that the domino men shut down all their moaning and complaining as soon as Lola came into the store. When she came in and greeted everyone with, "How y'all doin'" they knew it was not a greeting, but a trick question. So they kept her at bay by responding with a chorus of "We're just fine," and "Couldn't be better, Lola."

Once when I was suffering through "the curse" of my monthly malady, Mama made a big mistake. Without thinking about the consequence of sharing anything with Lola about pain or sickness and suffering, Mama let slip that I was "under the weather" a common euphemism that lent itself to no literal translation, but often meant, for females, "she's having her period."

I was lying on the sofa, trying hard not to throw up again when I heard Mama and Lola coming toward the house from the store. Mama knew by then that she'd made a serious mistake. Lola was marching across the yard like a crazed saint hell bent on healing an invalid or saving an infidel or casting out more demon fur balls. She was praying and moaning and making guttural sounds like the holy rollers in Uncle Wamon's church. Mama tried to stop her before she got to the door, but Mama was Southern in her soul and she could not bring herself to break the first commandment of Southern hospitality: "Thou shalt always make guests feel welcome." Lola was heading for the house un-invited, and Mama could not bring herself to stop her.

So Lola hit the front porch unchecked. It was summer time and only the screen door was closed. She opened it. Let it slam behind her. Then paused just inside the door. Ordinarily Lola had no internalized scruples, mores, or unwritten codes of behavior of any kind to slow her down, but just inside the door, she looked startled for a moment, as if in a brief flash of sanity, it dawned on her that she had just marched into Miz Meese's living room – uninvited .

She stopped yelping and moaning, got real quiet and tip-toed over to the couch. She looked down at me. I looked up at her. I needed to vomit. She needed to cast out demons. She bent over me, put her hand on my stomach before I could stop her and started moaning. I looked over at Mama. Her mouth was wide open and her lips were moving. She was obviously trying to speak, but no sound was coming out.

When I realized what Lola was intent on doing, I decided the best way to deal with her and get rid of her would be to let her succeed. So as Lola mumbled gibberish, I opened my eyes real wide and stared at the ceiling as if transfixed. I held that pose for a second and then suddenly sat bolt upright, and yelled,

"Watch out Lola – here comes the Holy Ghost!"

Just as suddenly as I sat up, I fell back again, shut my eyes, and made my body go stiff and rigid, which made me start shudder-ing and shaking. Then I sat up again and whispered with all the fervor and intensity I could muster,

"Stand back, Lola, I think the Devil's coming out of me!" I exhaled, sank back on the sofa and turned away from Lola because I couldn't keep a straight face any longer.

Lola was ecstatic. She started talking in tongues in earnest, punctuating the nonsense syllables with hallelujahs and amens. Then she started thanking the Lord and looking all around me to see if I had spit out any hairballs.

Mama recovered first, thanked her, took her arm and led her back outside. Then she came back in, sat down beside me and we started laughing and couldn't stop. I don't know whether it was Lola's intercession or Mama's laughing which always made me feel good or just that for a moment I stopped thinking about the nausea and it went away, but I did feel better and I got up and went to the door and watched Lola walking down the road. By the way she was walking, half-strutting, half-marching, you could tell she was really proud of what she had just done.

I guess the road from faith healer to whore is a pretty slippery slope, because not long after Lola cast out my devils, she gave up her healing ministry and, as they say in Baptist circles, started backsliding big time. Not so much because she lost her love for Jesus, but because of economic necessity. Without Red, Lola had only one marketable commodity and without Red, she also had no transportation. The only thing he left her that had wheels and an engine was an old John Deere tractor mower, so she started riding that to town every Saturday afternoon, parking it behind Marshall's diner, and walking around town doing her best to shake her hips, pooch out her lips and look seductive.

This was no easy task. Her liabilities included her heft, her hair, her teeth, and her preference for gaudy clothes. Still she managed a couple of times a Saturday to get herself picked up and driven off to give someone pleasure for money. Willy Ray and Billy Ray Martin, the pulpwood-logging twins were regulars.

In the course of marketing her only marketable commodity, Lola got pregnant, by God only knows who. As it gradually became obvious that Lola was "showing," everybody who came in the store started speculating about who was the daddy of Lola Smith's baby. Everybody talked about it, but no one dared to look her in the eye and ask. There was an unwritten rule that "thou shalt not look a woman in the eye and ask "who's the father of your child?" unless you were married to her or related by blood.

Lola never did eat right, but after she got pregnant, Mama, who was herself no exemplar of healthy choices in her own kitchen, tried harder than ever to talk to Lola about eating vegetables. She was encouraged when Lola announced she was going to plant a garden like Daddy's.

Daddy was a master gardener. He had a perfect garden. His rows had to be plumb-line straight, weeds were plucked as soon as they broke surface, and he picked things in patterns to maintain the symmetry of his rows. He'd pick every third onion even if it wasn't ready just to keep the gaps between his onions evenly spaced.

Mama wanted Daddy to talk to Lola about planting a garden. I think deep down my Daddy with his Quaker roots believed that talking was a sin. Mama and Aunt Velma, who was married to Daddy's baby brother, accepted the fact that in marrying Meese men they had waived the right ever to have a real conversation. It was hard to get Daddy to talk long about anything with anybody and near impossible to get him to even speak to Lola, but Mama nagged him until he gave in and agreed to walk her through his garden and show her his vegetables. She paid attention for as long as a woman with Adult Attention Deficit Disorder could and went back home inspired.

The next day she put on a big straw hat and got out an old hoe. She stood and stared at the ground for a while, picked up the hoe and whacked at the dirt for a few minutes. Then she sat down on her steps and lit a cigarette. She got up, turned over a little more dirt and went in the house and got a Coca Cola. All in all she dug, smoked and sipped for about an hour. Then she threw some seed on the ground and turned on the hose and washed most of them away. But she seemed pretty satisfied and proud of herself when she came back to the store. She sat down by Mama on the blue bench.

"I did it, Miss Maye," she announced. "I planted me a garden."

"Well, I saw you out there working, Lola, what did you plant?" Mama asked her, anticipating that Lola would someday have beans and peas and squash and okra, some real vegetables to supplement her usual diet of baloney and cheese.

"I planted all my fav'rites, Miss Maye – watermelon, cantaloupe, and peanuts. I "wontid" to plant some sugar cane, but they didn't have no sugar cane seed." Mama's shoulders sagged a little – defeated. Lola had planted the dream garden of children and sugar-lovers everywhere, but no vegetables.

Lola's craving for sugar was voracious. Undoubtedly she was an undiagnosed diabetic. As a result of her long belief that milk would constipate you, and her generally poor personal dental hygiene habits, her mouth was full of rotten teeth. Actually, she had a mouth full of black cavities held together with bits of yellowed enamel. Somehow, she had managed to hang on to a little bit of each of the two big ones in front. Until she got pregnant.

One day in about her seventh month, she came in to buy some candy. She said she was craving sugar. As usual she stood and stared at the candy display case as if she'd never been in the store before. It was the usual familiar country store stuff: Butterfingers, Baby Ruths, Jaw Breakers, peanut brittle….

"What kind you want today, Lola?

"Well, I *want* me one of them peanut brittle clusters", she said, "but I gotta have something I can suck on." With that, she grinned and opened her mouth and pointed to the empty space where her front teeth had been.

Standing before me was a middle-aged fat woman, made heavier still from carrying the fruit of her couplings with God only knew who. She sported a cap of frizzy fried hair, mostly gray now that the days of her bottle blondness were over and on this particular day, she'd made a couple of shaped spit curls that were held together with silver bobby pins on her forehead and in front of her ears. I think it was the spit curls that made me want to cry. They said to me that Lola, crazy, pregnant Lola still had some pride and still wanted to look pretty. Now she was standing there actually posing for me, flashing her snaggle-toothed smile without a hint of self-consciousness or embarrassment.

"What happened to your teeth, Lola?" I asked.

"I went to Dr. Thompson. He's gonna make me some of them pretty snow white ones. So, I reckon I'll have me some of them melty peppermint balls" she said in a tone that suggested she thought I would be impressed that she had made a healthy choice of candy. I didn't give much thought to the importance of dental hygiene either, but even I caught the irony of following the sentence, "I just went to the dentist" with "*soooo* I reckon I'll have me some melty peppermint balls."

I counted out ten penny peppermint balls with pale pinkish red stripes that melted when they got wet and gave them to her in a little brown paper bag. She popped one into each cheek and smiled again. Like a baby whose Mama had just dipped her pacifier in honey, Lola was satisfied.

But I was disturbed, because I couldn't figure out why seeing Lola so happy made me feel so sad.

There were all kinds of speculation about how we would come to find out who fathered Lola's baby. Mama said, "the way she is, we'll know when she names it because she'll name it after him, especially if it's a boy." Junior Cato figured we wouldn't know until the kid was old enough to tell who it looked like. Having personally seen her with the Case twins, I figured she'd have twin boys and name them Willy and Billy, though I hoped for the baby's sake that it didn't "take after" them because they were rough as corn cobs.

As it turned out, everybody was wrong. The baby looked exactly like Lola and she named him Elvis Presley Junior. Whoever the father was, he never came around or acknowledged his son, but, to his credit, he, or one of her other regulars, got tired of seeing her ride her lawn mower to town and gave her an old beat up Henry J.

It was hard to tell which she loved most – the car, her goat, or Elvis. She toted Elvis everywhere she went and the goat followed her everywhere she toted Elvis. She even took the back seat out of the Henry J so the goat, which she called Poot because he smelled so bad, could ride with her and Elvis. From some dormant sense of propriety or the lack of customers, after Elvis was born, nobody saw her streetwalking in Brookhaven again, but she still went to town every Saturday, and every Saturday she came back to the store with twenty five one dollar bills.

For the next few months, Lola settled into a routine that verged on normalcy. She walked her baby and her goat, she sat on her front steps singing to her baby and her goat, she sat in the corner and talked to Mama and Mr. DuBose and played with her baby like it was a doll. She never even tried to bring the goat in the store. Somehow she had enough sense to know that Daddy wouldn't allow it. Instead, she chained Poot to the front bumper of the Henry J and that goat would sit down on his hind haunches and wait for her like a dog. When she left, she'd buy him a moon pie and the three of them would go in the house and watch TV. I guess technically living with a goat and a mad mama made Elvis an abused child, but I know for a fact that his mama loved him to death.

One day a car a drove up in Lola's front yard. You could tell just by looking at it that it was some kind of "official business" car, the same way you can spot FBI agents by the color and fit of their suits and Mormon missionary boys who wear long sleeved white shirts and neckties while riding bicycles. A man and a woman with high-heeled shoes on got out and went in Lola's house. They came back out in a little while holding Elvis and a big brown paper bag. They got in their car and left, and nobody ever saw or heard of him again. Lola didn't try to stop them or anything. She stood in the yard and watched them leave, and then went back and sat down on her top step and put her head down in her hands and just sat there.

Eulogies for Lola and Fonnie

When they took Elvis away from Lola, Mama was conflicted. On one hand she had worried about Elvis' well-being from the time she first knew Lola had a baby in her womb. She knew that raising a baby and a goat as siblings was bad parenting, and she knew that as soon as Elvis got enough teeth, Lola would start feeding him Moon Pies and RC Colas and stop giving him milk so he wouldn't get constipated. On the other hand Mama was herself one of those possessive-I-just-live-for-my-baby kind of mothers. She couldn't empathize with Lola when she was a shopaholic, a touch healer and a whore, but she knew in her very soul how lost Lola must be after somebody drove off with Elvis and left her alone.

Old man Fonnie Dubose, who'd never, as far as he knew, fathered a child, shared Mama's concerns. He ached for Lola and tried to comfort her when she came and sat with him in the corner of the store.

Lola mourned for Elvis and stayed on the down slope of a depressive cycle for months though she never explained where he went. Then one day she burst into the store in high manic mode and announced that she was gonna start bootlegging. From time to time Lola had spells of lucidity and flashes of the cunning and shrewdness of a real entrepreneur, though usually her efforts to think her way down a chain of logical necessity were based on false premises and thus led to flawed conclusions.

Back behind our house, Mama and Daddy had once put in spaces for ten trailers to park, thinking to make a little extra money from renting to the peripatetic oil field roughnecks who drove past the store every day. It was the shrewdest business plan Daddy ever had. He figured he could rent the spaces and get an on-the-premises customer base to buy their food and gas and cigarettes at the store.

It didn't work out that way though. The trailer park never had more than three or four renters at any one time. We wound up with riff-raff in our back yard who made too much noise, left beer bottles every where, stole socks off Mama's clothes line, charged everything they took out of the store and pulled out in the middle of the night without paying their bills and headed down the road to Enterprise or back to Texas to dig some more dry holes. Daddy finally shut down the trailer park to cut his losses.

But Daddy made an exception for Mr. Dubose whom we sort of inherited when his half-sister and only living relative moved to Jackson and left him. Fonnie Dubose lived in a little teeny-weeny camping trailer. For a few years, he'd parked it down the road at his sister's house. I never understood why he wanted to be close to his sister in the first place because he didn't seem to like her or her husband or her children, and she just completely ignored him. As far as I know, he never set foot in her house and she never went past his front door, preferring to stand outside his little trailer and holler at him when she had something to tell him.

Fonnie had once had copper toned red hair, but now it was so flecked with white that it looked pink. I told him one time, as a compliment, that I thought his hair was the color of a strawberry roan horse. Somehow he thought it hilarious that I'd told him he had hair like a horse and he laughed and laughed and never forgot it. He loved to tell people that I said he looked like a horse.

One of Fonnie's eye sockets was empty and he wore glasses with one frosted and one clear lens. It didn't look too funny when you looked at him straight on from the front, but when you sat beside him, you could see what a big hole he had in his face. Store regulars and the domino men never mentioned it, but once a little boy came in the store, stared at Mr. Dubose, sidled around to get a look behind the frosted lens and blurted out,

"Hey, mister, where's your other eye?"

All Fonnie said was, "Had an accident." He never explained further and we didn't ask.

What Mr. Dubose did every day was get up, make himself a cup of coffee, dress, get his walking cane, and walk up to the store. In the winter, he sat in the chair closest to the heater, and in the summer, he sat outside on the blue bench. He sat there and read the paper, ate a cinnamon roll or powdered doughnut, and made conversation with everyone who came to the store. At noon be bought some cheese and crackers, walked back down the road, ate, took a nap and walked back to the store and sat in the corner until we got ready to close. Then he bought a can of tomato or chicken noodle soup, walked back home, ate the soup and went to bed. The next day he did the same thing and the day after that he did the same thing again.

When his sister's husband got a job in Jackson, the Jordans sold their place and moved. Apparently they didn't properly ask Fonnie to move along with them like they really wanted him to. They told him he could come if he wanted to and they'd let him put his trailer in their backyard. Fonnie's feelings were hurt and he was stompin' mad. "If they don't want me," he said, "they can just go straight to hell!" He said Mama and Daddy and I, who spent all day long every day with Fonnie Dubose, were more his family anyway.

So when the Jordans left town, Daddy hooked up Fonnie's

trailer and hauled it down to the back of our now defunct trailer park and Fonnie lived in our back yard until he died. His routine changed a little bit after we adopted him. To maintain his independence and because he could, he still made his own coffee and heated his own soup, but Mama insisted that he eat dinner with us.

Like a chameleon, Fonnie had a wonderful ability to take on the color of the background wherever he sat down. That is, he related to and connected with everyone he met – on their terms. When he was alone in the store with my Daddy, they just sat and rocked, Fonnie matching Daddy silence for silence, monosyllable for monosyllable. It wasn't that Daddy didn't like Mr. Dubose. He loved him. He just treated everyone as if they were at a Quaker meeting waiting to see who would speak first and vowing that it wouldn't be him.

When Fonnie and Mama were alone in the store, they nearly gossiped themselves to death. Between the two of them, nothing going on within five miles of the store went unnoticed. Mama still went to town and played canasta or rook with "the girls," but Fonnie Dubose became her best friend and confidante, the perfect anti-Daddy as a conversationalist.

When I kept the store, Fonnie let me drive the conversation. We mostly talked about my trick horse, Slim, my shy boyfriend, Soren, my homework, or my friends and teachers. Fonnie was interested in it all. But sometimes I had the good sense to shut up and ask Fonnie about where he'd been and what he'd seen. He fascinated me because he was one of the few people I'd ever known who: (a) wasn't born in Mississippi, (b) had been all the way through four years of college, and (c) had traveled everywhere, building things.

Mr. Dubose's good eye really did twinkle all the time. He was the oldest frailest man I knew, yet he had the look and the mindset of a mischievous boy who was always on the verge of playing a prank on you. He was perpetually bemused by life as it unfolded around him in his corner in the country store. Like a kid with an ant farm who relished standing on the outside watching scurrying ants through the glass even when they tried to hide in their subterranean tunnels, Fonnie was an "experience voyeur," who could have found no better place on earth for observing the human scene and living vicariously through others than from his corner in our country store in South Mississippi in the mid 50s.

Lola was one of his favorite ants. He loved watching her. He loved talking to her. When the woman in the high heeled shoes took Elvis and Lola sat on her steps and mourned, Fonnie ached with her. But he was no more successful than the rest of us when he tried to talk sense to Lola and make sense of the things she did. Some of her wilder schemes actually revealed that somewhere in the recesses of her splintered brain, there was an incipient entrepreneur. Her honky-tonk plan, for example. The day she burst back into the store in full blown manic mode announcing her intention to be a bootlegger, she ran over to Fonnie, too excited to sit still, and said,

"Guess what, Mr. Fonnie, I'm gonna build me a honky-tonk."

Mama gasped. Daddy cursed under his breath and walked out. Fonnie didn't even blink his good eye.

"But, Miss Lola," he reminded her, "Mississippi is a dry state. It's illegal to sell whiskey and if you start bootlegging over there, Sheriff Brueck will come out here and arrest you. And you know you can't have a honky-tonk without selling whiskey." Lola usually responded to logic by withdrawing into petulant silence. That day, it didn't faze her.

"Well, Mr. Fonnie," she said, "the sheriff ain't gonna know it's a honky-tonk." She paused, "cause I'm gonna put a picture of Jesus in the window and I'm gonna hide the house."

Mama and Daddy usually didn't get too upset about Lola's schemes because they knew she'd either forget the next day and move on to something else or be stymied by her own inability to accomplish anything more complicated than eating and walking her goat at the same time.

That changed the next day when they looked across the road and saw that she had propped up a huge picture of Jesus in the front window.

They began to really get worried when she got out Red's old tools and started cutting down all the scrub pines around the house. She'd cut one down and then take it over and lean it against the side of the house. By the end of the week, her whole yard had been denuded, pine stumps were sticking up everywhere, and she had completely covered the front, back and sides of her house with leaning pine trees.

She'd done exactly what she'd told us she was going to do. She'd hidden her house. Only the low-slung blue roof was sticking up out of the green pine boughs. It was actually kind of pretty until all the green dried up and everything turned brown.

The picture of Jesus stayed in the window for a few months, the wind blew most of the pines down and after awhile Lola stopped talking about her honky-tonk, but her behavior became increasingly bizarre.

One day when Mama, Daddy, Fonnie, the domino men and I were all in the store, Lola came out in her yard carrying her record player. It was a pretty nice one – one that she had bought when she was married and spending Red's money. She went back in and came back out again with an armload of records. She set them down and went over to the side of the house and turned on the hose like she was going to get a drink of water. Instead, she turned the hose on the record player and filled it full of water. Then she picked up the records, went over and stood on the edge of her yard and started hurling country western records like black vinyl Frisbees at passing cars. The people in the cars looked startled, the domino men started laughing, but Fonnie Dubose shook his head, sadly. He realized that Lola's acceleration into pure madness was now in over-drive.

After the record tossing episode, talk cranked up around the store about *somebody* needing to do *something*. The domino men usually followed *something* with *"about* Lola." Mama and Fonnie talked instead about doing *something "for"* her. A prepositional distinction of real significance.

In fact, reactions to "Lola the Mad Woman of Enterprise Road" began to break along gender lines. The men, threatened by the sight of a crazy woman continued to ridicule her and wanted her punished.

"If she ever th'ows somethin' at my car, I'm callin' Joe Brueck."

"That woman ought to be put in Whitfield and locked up till the devil comes to git her."

"It's a good thing for Old Red that he got out while the gittin' was good."

Women, on the other hand, were more inclined to be sympathetic, but from a distance. For them, Lola was kind of like a mangy dog. You might feel sorry for it, but you wouldn't want to touch it. When women saw her coming they would duck their heads and run get in their cars without making eye contact or saying a word to her.

Mama and Fonnie thought Lola needed to be sent to Whitfield, the state run all-purpose mental hospital and addiction center, not to punish her, but to get her help. Trouble was, neighbors didn't have a legal right to cart neighbors off to an insane asylum, and her siblings stopped having anything to do with her right after Elvis was born. It wasn't an act of moral piety – they had relatives all over Lincoln County of dubious parentage. It was because she embarrassed them by naming her son of sin after Elvis Presley.

Mama thought about calling Lola's sisters who lived out in a little communal cluster north of McComb. But she didn't. The mores of our community were known and understood by every man, woman, and child. Everybody left everything unlocked all the time and it was o.k. to go into your neighbor's house when they weren't home to use their phone if you didn't have one, or to borrow an egg or some milk if you didn't have time to go to the store.

But you didn't ever – ever – ever butt into their private business.

If a husband came home drunk and passed out in the front yard, you pretended not to see him. If a woman showed up with a black eye and a bruised face, you pretended to believe her when she said she stepped on a rake and it popped up and hit her in the nose or she reached on the top shelf for something and a jar of pickle relish fell and hit her in the face.

So Mama was in a quandary. She was afraid to call Lola's sisters and tell them they needed to do something about their sister, and she was afraid not to.

The Easter Bunny episode helped Mama make up her mind.

The scene. Mama was out in the yard raking and burning some pine straw. The domino men were playing outside. Daddy was sitting on the blue bench. I was playing with Slim. The Enterprise school bus was stopped across the road. It was the last day of school before Easter Sunday. Back then Easter was a pretty big holiday in Mississippi, celebrated with huge Easter baskets filled with candy and stuffed animals and live baby chicks and ducks and rabbits for the kids, a prayer service for Jesus at sunrise and dozens of deviled eggs for dinner.

Lola celebrated it a bit differently that year. She tried to *become* the Easter bunny. She got a pink fuzzy blanket, cut out a couple of eye holes so she could see, put it over her head, tied a big pink bow around her neck and stuck a big ball of cotton on her backside to complete the Peter Cottontail look. She walked to the edge of her yard, put her hands together in front of her, bent her wrists down, assumed a rabbit pose and started hopping down the road.

The school bus driver, initially stopped for a passing car, stayed stopped at the sight of the pink-clad-rabbit-hopping Lola.

Lola kept on hopping until she got across the road. Then she lay down and started rolling like a log. She rolled down our gravel driveway. She rolled across our front yard. She rolled straight toward Mama and right through the burning pine needles. Then she rolled down the hill all the way to the briar patch at the edge of the pasture.

The whole thing lasted only a few minutes, but it seemed to play out in slow motion. Nobody moved or said anything, not even the kids on the school bus who usually snickered and pointed and whispered when they saw Lola. This time they just leaned against the windows and gawked.

When she could roll no farther, Lola got up, adjusted her pink blanket so she could see out of the eyeholes, hopped back to her house and went inside. Silence. Then one of the domino men said, "It's your play," the school bus driver put the bus in gear and turned left. And Mama went inside and called Lola's sister.

They must have come that very same night, too embarrassed to be seen in broad daylight. Lola never came back to live in the house on Enterprise Road. When Highway 84 came through, that corner was cut off and the house knocked down. Now everybody who wants to get from Natchez to Monticello drives right through the middle of the house where Lola's honky-tonk never stood.

You might be tempted to believe that the Gothic characters you see in the movies with bad bad southern accents are the products of the alcohol induced dementia of failed novelists turned B-movie screenwriters. But the South I grew up in *was* peopled with characters like Lola and Fonnie. They walked into and out of my Daddy's little country store every day of the week. They were the stuff of Truman and Tennessee and Willie and Eudora's fiction and they were the stuff of my southern fried life and every day reality.

Of all the characters I remember from growing up in Brookhaven, Mississippi, Lola Smith was the most unforgettable. After I left home and went off to college and a life in academia,

I often asked Mama when we talked on the phone, "Well, have you heard anything about Lola?"

And Mama would tell me she'd heard Lola was in Whitfield or out again, or back in again. Then I heard nothing about her for a long time.

A couple of years later when I called Mama to make plans for Christmas vacation, she stopped in mid sentence and said,

"Oh, I heard Lola Smith died." Period. End of a life. End of story? Not really. For reasons I couldn't begin to fathom, I was inconsolably saddened by news of Lola's death. She still looms large in my memory as the iconic symbol of insanity – the face of madness. In an odd way I'm humbled by knowing that I may well be the only person on earth to remember and write a eulogy for Lola.

Lola brought color and drama and humor into my life and the lives of the characters who gathered in Daddy's store to watch her through our store windows from time to time. There were so many facets to her personality and so many phases of her life that I'm hard pressed to find a summative word – an epitaph for Lola. She was impulsive, delusional, sinful, simple, cunning and resourceful. But above all else, Lola was an optimist. She believed she could cure sick kittens and cast out devils and heal others and make them whole. She believed that if she put a picture of Jesus in her window, the sheriff wouldn't know she was building a honky-tonk. When she looked in the mirror, she still believed that she was beautiful. And in a way – a very strange way – she was.

Southern Fried Greece

The last place on earth one would have expected to find vestiges of a Greek chorus in the 1940s and 50s would have been Brookhaven, Mississippi. Loughlan Maclean Watt in an article on "Attic and Elizabethan Tragedy" wrote:

> ...The Chorus rejoiced in the triumph of good; it wailed aloud its grief, and sympathized with the woe of the puppets of the gods. It entered deeply into the interest of their fortunes and misfortunes, yet it stood apart, outside of triumph and failure.

By that definition, Brookhaven used to be full of Southern Fried Greek choruses and I knew everybody in at least three of them up close and personal: The Fire Station Guys, The Gossip Box and Canasta Gals, and The Domino Men.

After the war (WWII) started and fuel was scarce and gas was rationed, Daddy got out of the service station business for awhile because it was such a mess fooling with rationing stamps. He drove out to Texas and tried to get a job at a shipbuilding yard, but couldn't and came back to Brookhaven after just a few days and got a job as a fireman. There were two apartments upstairs over the fire station. Red Meyers, the Fire Chief and his wife, Miss Mary, lived in one and Mama and Daddy and I moved into the other one. The third full-time fireman was an old German bachelor named Fritz Tools who lived in a tiny dark room in the basement of the station.

Living at the fire station came with some built in perks. I got to ride on the fire truck when it went out for parades and non-emergencies. I got to fill the auxiliary tank back up with water when the truck returned from a small fire. And I got to play cards and checkers and dominoes with the Fire Station guys.

There was a cadre of regulars, who hung out at the fire station all day long, every day. There were no able-bodied young regulars. They were all off in the war, so the regulars were retired old men or worthless men who were too lazy to work or claimed to be too sick to work, but not sick enough to stay home in bed. The old men sat in wooden high straight-backed chairs and tilted them backwards to lean against the brick walls so their front chair legs and their feet were off the ground. Some chewed tobacco and spat with varying degrees of accuracy toward an empty tin bucket. They read the newspaper, told each other lies about fish and women, and carried on a running commentary on local politics.

There was no such thing as a two-party system in Mississippi back then. They were all Democrats. And Patriots. And hypocrites. They hated Hitler and the "*Natzis*" as they pronounced it, not because they were killing Jews, but because they were killing "our boys." They cussed the Sheriff for being a crook, but kept on voting for the ones that protected their favorite bootlegger.

They had what I can now only describe as some kind of old man male bonding ritual. When they first got to the fire station in the morning they were stone silent. First one, then the other, would come in, look around, do a quick nose count, bob his head and grunt a greeting, drag up a chair, and get out his favorite nicotine fix. Then they would sit there and dip, chaw, puff, spit and cough for a while like members of a chorus warming up with their individual riffs before everyone started singing together. It was as if they had a gentleman's agreement not to start anything recognizable as a conversation until everyone got there – unlike Mama's gossip box and canasta playing friends who started talking as soon as they saw the white of a friend's eyes and kept on talking non-stop until they were out of sight.

Big Bill, another regular, had smoked the most Camel cigarettes and coughed the most, and because he had once run for public office, was deferred to as authority on anything that smacked of politics. He was also a master of all firehouse games: Setback, gin, dominoes and checkers.

Because there were no other children living at the fire station, the old men were my playmates. They taught me all their games and when they were a player short invited me to play with them. Bless their hearts, when everything in them must have been straining to punctuate their stories with profanity, they watched their language, refrained from the "God damns" and "sons-of-bitches" and kept their plain *damns* and *hells* to a minimum when they knew I was around.

Mama and her three best friends – Cathleen "Cat" Jackson, married to Dewey, who worked for Uncle Frank; Josie Barlow, married to Mr. Barlow, the District Attorney (I don't know if he had a first name or not. If he did, nobody called him by it. Even Josie called him Mr. Barlow), and Irma Foster who was married to Vernon, who didn't do anything but sit around Pitt's Taxi stand and pretend he worked there – did their choral commentary in two arenas – what they called the gossip box at the Brookhaven Specialty Shop and at their weekly canasta game. The contrast between the old men's chorus and the women's chorus couldn't have been more stark. Mama and her friends never talked about politics or world affairs. They talked about people. About people they liked and people they didn't like and people who were sick and people who were dying. They shook their heads over tales of sorry two-timing men . They ooohed and aaahed over pretty babies and not so pretty ones too and once a week they got together and played canasta and had an uninterrupted talkathon, which Irma especially enjoyed. It really annoyed her when they would be right at a critical point in a conversation in the gossip box and she'd have to get up and go wait on a customer and miss the punch line of a joke or a critical part of the story.

To me Cat was the most interesting of Mama's friends. She didn't have any teeth. Well, she had some false ones, but couldn't or wouldn't wear them, and her lips and chin were sunken in so far they were almost gone and it made a funny curve. Most people with false teeth are embarrassed about being seen without their dentures. Once when Mama's false teeth broke, she held her hand in front of her mouth all day long and wouldn't go outside or let anyone see her until her teeth were fixed. I was embarrassed too. Not because of the way she looked, but because she made me take her teeth in a paper bag to Dr. Ripley to stick them back together, and I felt really strange walking through the streets of Brookhaven totin' my Mama's teeth in a paper bag.

Cat wasn't embarrassed at all. She didn't hold her hand in front of her mouth or anything, and what was really strange was that she liked to have her picture taken and when she did – she smiled with her mouth open so you could see her gums – gums as tough as corn cobs. Without any teeth, Cat couldn't even bite a biscuit, but once she got something in her mouth, she could gum and suck just about anything to mush.

One night, when she was in her early 40s and sitting at the canasta table with Mama and Josie and Irma, she fell forward on the card table and died right then and there. Had a heart attack and was taken away to Uncle Frank's embalming room and prepared for visitation and viewing. Word was that the beautician to the un-living had a terrible time trying to figure out where to put the red lipstick on Cat who in death had no lips at all. Everybody who paid their respects to Cat remarked that Dewey the griever's grief, seemed real for the first time ever. He cried. That would have made Cat really happy because she never believed Dewey cared anything about her at all. She told Mama and Irma that all the time.

When we moved to the country and Daddy built his little combination country store and service station, he didn't realize that he was also building a community center, but in effect, that's what he did. In the 40s and 50s, country stores were magnets that brought together friends and neighbors from miles around.

Almost as soon as the store opened, a chorus began to form.

Daddy realized the value of having customers come and stick around the store and did his best to accommodate them. He set up a card table and put in a few chairs over by the space-heater in the corner of the store and he built a bench outside between a couple of scrub oak trees and painted it Pure Oil blue. The table became home base for the basses and Mama and the sopranos and a few altos held court outside on the blue bench. In the summer the men moved their table out of their cramped corner and set up their table outside too.

While the old men at the fire station talked about politics, and war and football and hunting dogs and the gossip box women covered miscarriages, drunk husbands, clothes and Brother Miller's sermons, the chorus at the store carved out a different niche. They were mostly farmers, dairymen, oil field workers, and truck drivers with an occasional lazy lout or two. They talked a lot about the weather and corn and cotton and cows and the price of chicken feed and Lola Smith. The women outside on the blue bench with Mama mostly talked about their children and their gardens and canning pickles and casserole recipes and potted plants and Lola Smith.

Though I was a child when I listened to the choruses, for the most part as an observer, not a participant, I realize that I absorbed something from all of them. Collectively they added the seasoning to my southern fried childhood and shaped the adult I have become.

Epilogue

*O*ne of the requirements for the second doctoral program I began, but didn't finish, was fifteen hours of eight hundred level statistics. I dreaded it. I wasn't math phobic – didn't fear it – just hated it. I began the first class with only a fuzzy notion of the difference between medium, mean and mode. I made 15 hours of "A" and at the end of the last class still had only a fuzzy notion of the difference between medium, mean and mode. I didn't learn anything about statistics.

I did learn one very valuable lesson about teaching and learning from that experience. I learned that it is possible to make an "A" without learning anything. From that I reasoned that it is also possible to learn a lot and still make a "D" or an "F". And from that I reasoned that giving tests and exams to my students was at best an inexact and unreliable way to measure student learning.

From that point on, in every class I taught, I spent an hour or so asking my students one simple and direct question: *"What have you learned* in this class this quarter? Anything? Not just from the lectures or the book – but *anything."* Students always loved the exercise and the discussions that followed were sometimes surprising and provocative and always revealing. I could never have constructed a test or exam with questions to elicit the answers that the question "What have you learned?" got out of them, and the exercise itself proved to be a valuable learning experience. As one student would weigh in with "I learned..." you could see another student go "aha, I learned that too!"

At the end of the hour, I suggested that my students ask themselves that question every night. Over the years many of them have come back to thank me and tell me how much they learned by consciously and deliberately processing their experiences through the filter of the question. "What have I leaned today?"

I didn't set out to write a book with lessons and Aesop's Fables kind of morals for the reader. And I am not going to do that now.

But I have asked myself the logical question: "what have I learned from writing this book?"

My answer surprised me. I thought I might have learned a lot about myself, but I really didn't. *I learned that nothing we can do is more important than remembering the past because as the tide of time moves us inexorably forward much of what we leave behind is lost – forever.*

Of course I knew that things change – that every day the world is a new and different place, but I didn't realize until the theme emerged in this book just how soon after things are gone, they can be completely obliterated and – forgotten. Clare Harvey's sharecropper shack, Lola's might-have-been a honky-tonk house, an entire creek that ran under the bridge where we caught back-scooting crawdads – all gone. And not *just* gone, but evidence that they were ever there as undetectable as if they never existed.

Important and inconsequential people alike lived and died in Brookhaven, Mississippi, and are now almost entirely forgotten. And when those of us who still remember them are gone – they will be entirely forgotten.

Children cannot remember what they never knew and they cannot know – really know what they have not experienced. I believe we have a duty to remember and to share our memories. I set out to write a book to leave memories of me for my children, but I learned that I want a whole lot more than that remembered.

I knew so many others who deserve to be remembered. I want an old red haired man named Fonnie Dubose and a crazy woman named Lola to be remembered. I want a magnificent horse that died in a pasture in Bogue Chito and an old cobbler named Mr. Lankford who trusted everything he owned to a ten year old child to be remembered. I want a young nun who laughed and skipped like a child to be remembered.

I want my Mama and Daddy to be remembered, and, yes, I want to be remembered too.

So, now I have entrusted my memories to you. I want you to remember my memories, but because of what I know about the limits of human communication – I know you can't. Still, I hope you will try.

Remember....

About the Author

Jimmie Meese Moomaw was "born and raised" in Brookhaven, Mississippi. Named by her Daddy eighteen years before she was born, she grew up as the only child of alcoholic parents in the Deep South during the 40s and 50s.

Though she left Mississippi in the 60s to go to graduate school in Illinois, she never lost touch with her Southern roots. At the end of the "Prologue" to *Southern Fried Child*, she wrote: "I'll never know for sure who or what I might have been or would have been if I had been born in Connecticut or Detroit, but I am now sure that I am who I am in large measure because I was born in "Home Seeker's Paradise" and lived a Southern fried childhood, complete with horses and healers and heathens and whores and flawed parents who loved me both too much and not enough."

Moomaw taught Communication on the college and university level for 40 years. Now retired from teaching, she is a political consultant, writer and popular public speaker living in Avondale Estates, Georgia.

LaVergne, TN USA
13 December 2010
208581LV00014B/121/P